SCHOLASTIC

MW01057039

Writing to Prompts
for Success *on the* Test

MARY ROSE

Dedication The Teachers at Phyllis Wheatley Elementary School in Apopka, Florida. This was a group of amazing administrators, fabulous teachers, strong women, and great friends. I am a better person and a better teacher because of their influences on my life. I couldn't list everyone, but I especially want to recognize Elaine Apter, Charlotte Campbell (deceased), Janice Dorminey, Janet Foster, Karen Fritz, Carolyn Hauser, Leon Henderson, Clair Hoey, Dian Hooper, Jean Howe, Leonard Ingram (deceased), Jan Lawhorn, Hilda Leudenburg, Brenda Mizell, Doris Pruett, Beverly Richardson, Karen Robinson, Laurie Skinner, Sandra Smith (deceased), Gail Terry, Margaret Terry, Betty Wilson, and Claudia Worthington.

Thanks to several parents who gave permission to use their children's work in this book. Special thanks go to Glen, Jodi, and Jenna Jaffee for generously allowing me to use several of Jenna's essays as examples of fourth-grade writing skills. Thanks also to Virginia Dooley and Mela Ottaiano of Scholastic Inc.

Editor: Mela Ottaiano
Cover design: Wendy Chan
Interior design: Melinda Belter
Interior illustrations: Teresa Anderko
ISBN: 978-0-545-23459-7
Copyright © 2011 by Scholastic Inc.
All rights reserved. Published by Scholastic Inc.
Printed in the U.S.A.
1 2 3 4 5 6 7 8 9 10   40   17 16 15 14 13 12 11

New York • Toronto • London • Auckland • Sydney **Teaching**
Mexico City • New Delhi • Hong Kong • Buenos Aires *Resources*

Contents

Introduction

Almost every state now assesses students' writing in elementary school, in middle school, and again in high school. Students are given a specific prompt and asked to respond with a narrative, an expository, a descriptive, or a persuasive essay. Because writing a persuasive essay is the most difficult, it is usually not tested until high school and therefore will not be covered here.

The aim of this book is to help teachers help students receive high scores on state writing assessments, but it is also intended to provide a foundation on which all future writing can be based. It is no coincidence that the creators of state assessments identified the most basic, necessary elements of writing and chose to evaluate student essays based on student ability to use them. Teachers have long known what to teach. This book provides "how to teach" and "what to use" to help students master the basics and become confident writers. It clarifies and simplifies state writing standards so that teachers can present each one and assure their students receive the highest scores possible.

Each of the five chapters focuses on a specific skill that students need in order to be successful writers. The first chapter contains background information, help with reading and interpreting a prompt, and help with creating graphic organizers. The second chapter is about introductions and closings. The third is the most important because it helps children with the main body of the essay. It also contains information about how to raise student scores above the minimum standard.

The fourth chapter is about using words wisely. This will help your students make their writing more interesting with details, a strong vocabulary, and figurative language. The last chapter is about editing and conventions of print. It also contains lessons on titling work, editing checklists, and guidelines for writing mentors. Finally, you will find a bank of narrative, expository, and descriptive writing prompts to provide students with plenty of practice. Every part of this book is, of course, useful to teachers and students that want to be better writers, even though they may not be facing a state assessment.

One of my former students, Jenna, has allowed me to use some of her essays as examples of quality student writing. Her writing is solid and likely would have received a "5" on the Florida Writing Assessment. Consider sharing these with your students to see if they can identify what makes these pieces strong.

I hope you enjoy this book and find its lessons helpful. Thanks to all of you for the hard work and dedication I know you give to your students. I admire each and every one of you for the amazing things you accomplish.

Mary

CHAPTER 1

Setting the Stage for Success

Writing is one of the most difficult tasks that we ask students to do. When we ask our students to write a story or an essay, they must use virtually every language and grammar skill they have ever been taught. They must decide on a topic, organize their thoughts, come up with a good introduction, remember what to capitalize, where to punctuate, how to use proper syntax, and how to be interesting at the same time. While our writers are doing this, they must also manipulate a pencil, stay between the lines on the paper, or "hunt and peck" on a keyboard. Writing is hard work. And students are even more intimidated when they know they are being judged on the quality of what they write. No wonder so many children (and adults) are stricken with acute writers' block.

Writing is also one of the most neglected areas of the curriculum. Most teachers have had extensive classes on how to teach social studies, science, reading, and math, but they have had little or no training on how to teach writing. Worst of all, when districts have adopted "writing curriculums" or when teachers have attended workshops about teaching writing, the writing instruction has centered on narrative writing and creative writing. In these workshops, teachers have been taught to establish writer's workshops, where students learn to plan, write, revise, and publish their short stories. They receive excellent instruction on how to craft creative paragraphs with great figurative language. But when students take the state writing assessment, many of them—even those whom teachers have deemed "great writers"—get poor marks. Why is this happening? Here are some of the reasons:

- Students who excel in writer's workshop usually self-select a topic, so they have not been taught to read, interpret, and respond to a specific prompt.

- Writer's workshop offers students opportunities to use a dictionary and a thesaurus. These are not usually permitted on state writing assessments.

- In writer's workshop, students may work for a week or two or even three on just one story. On state writing assessments, they must plan and write in about 45 minutes.

- Students in writer's workshop are used to having unlimited space for their stories. On most state writing assessments, students are given quite a limited space to write their essay, often only the front and back of one sheet of paper.

The language of writing assessments

State assessments, writing programs, and student textbooks often use different terminology, so make sure your students know that some words are interchangeable. This will help them understand directions for writing, no matter if they get a new teacher, move to a new state, or begin using new textbooks.

FOCUS The words *focus, main idea, topic,* and *subject* mean almost the same thing. When students are given a prompt, any of these four terms may be used to indicate the subject of the prompt. Help your students understand that *main idea, topic, subject,* and *focus* all refer to the same thing; they are not four different things they need to do!

Occasionally, students will lose their focus (also called getting off topic or not addressing the prompt). When this happens, the result is a poor score.

ORGANIZATION With few exceptions, every piece of writing incorporates an organizational plan. While many are acceptable, we like to stick with the basics in elementary school. Usually a scorer is looking for a clear introduction, a series of chronological events (in narrative writing) or reasons why (in expository or persuasive writing), supporting details or paragraphs of description, and a clear and connected closing.

The introduction is pretty much just referred to that way, but an ending can also be called a closing or a conclusion. The closing of a letter is where you write "Very truly yours" or "Sincerely" followed by your name.

SUPPORT Support is a critical component of any piece of writing, especially on a state writing assessment. Even if a student writes a weak introduction and closing, the scorers will take into account if the student uses strong supporting details. A strong essay will

have the word *describe* in the direction sentence. Students being tested on how to write a persuasive essay will find the words *convince* or *persuade* in the final sentence.

- Have students circle the clue words and the subject of the prompt.

- Reread the prompt. We usually recommend that students spend about five minutes reading the prompt and creating a graphic organizer as a plan. Part of the five minutes should be spent reading the prompt more than one time. It is also acceptable to have a moment of quiet "think time" before students grab a pencil and start a mad dash of writing.

- Students should learn to use the prompt to answer their own questions. If the prompt is "Write about a time you got a haircut," the child may be asking himself if he can write about a time his brother got a haircut or if he can write

have clearly written topic sentences, with supporting details, or "extensions," that follow. Chapter 2 contains good examples of this format. Every paragraph is three sentences long, with a topic sentence and two pieces of "support." (Note: The topic sentence does not have to be first. It is just as effective, and maybe even more so, when it is placed in the middle or at the end of a paragraph. Usually only the most capable writers can do this in elementary school.)

After the topic sentence and the extensions, authors often give examples that relate to the topic, write paragraphs of description, or put in a small vignette. These are called elaborations, and it is the elaboration paragraphs that usually raise a student's score on writing assessments.

Although technically they are each a little different, the terms *supporting details, extensions,* and *elaborations* are often used interchangeably with beginning writers.

CONVENTIONS OF PRINT Also called rules of grammar, or mechanics of language, conventions of print refers to both grammar (the system of rules by which words are formed and put together to make sentences) and mechanics (capitalization, spelling, punctuation, and other aspects that make our writing comprehensible).

CONVERSATION Make sure your students know the difference between a quotation and a whole conversation. A quotation can be one word, one sentence, one paragraph, or several paragraphs. Dialogue is a conversation, where two or more people are exchanging words. The words that tell who is speaking ("said Martha," "replied Janet") are called speech tags.

about a time he cut his brother's hair. A careful rereading will tell him that he should write about a time *he* got a haircut. Teach your students to reread the prompt to answer their own questions; you will not be allowed to help them on test day.

- Most elementary and middle school prompts ask for a personal narrative, so the child should be using "I," "we," and "us," not writing in the third person.

The prompts can be fiction or nonfiction—even expository essays. Once I had a student who was asked to write about how to be a good helper in the classroom. She wrote about how she would vacuum out the children's desks, set up an automatic mouse cage-cleaning machine, and stand on wet sponges as she skated around the classroom to scrub the floor. Outlandish, yes, but this was an excellent example of expository fiction, and her score was a 6.

Analytic vs. holistic scoring

Analytic scoring is when a piece of writing is "taken apart" and each element is awarded points depending on how well the child was able to incorporate these into the completed essay. A few states still use analytic scoring, so you may encounter a score of 4.23 on a child's work. Most states, however, score writing holistically. This means that the scorer considers the essay as a whole and awards a score based on his or her consideration of all the elements at the same time. Essays scored like this are given a whole number score, such as a 4. When papers are scored holistically but receive a number such as 4.5, this means that the paper was read two times and one scorer gave it a 4 and the other gave it a 5.

Making a Plan for Writing

Many teachers find it helpful to have students use a graphic organizer to organize their thoughts and plan their work, and there are dozens of clever and thoughtful organizers available for teachers to share with their students. But having too many choices is confusing for students who are not sophisticated enough to distinguish one "thinking design" from another. Keep it simple by choosing *one* organizer and using it for all kinds of writing: narrative, expository, descriptive, and persuasive.

Your students have probably already been exposed to graphic organizers, bubble maps, T-charts, and other kinds of planning devices. What they rarely understand is the real purpose of these planners and when to use each one.

Each graphic organizer used here (pages 12–14) essentially looks like a giant plus sign. This gives students a space to make notes for their introduction and closing, as well as areas to list the three main events in the story, the three reasons why or steps in a process, or three ways of describing something. Help your students understand that the information they put on this organizer will provide the basis for their topic sentences when they begin to write. This format is also very easy for students to recreate on their own.

Help for struggling and inexperienced writers

Your most at-risk students may not be able to complete these pages independently— at least not the first time or two. Plan to work through this page, one box at a time and when you're helping students think through reasons why, events in a story, or parts of description. When you first teach students how to do this, allow them at least 30 minutes just to complete the planning sheet. It also helps to model what you want them to do by completing an organizer of your own and writing a few notes in each box.

How to write a prompt

This book provides many prompts that you can use to prepare for state writing assessments and to help make writing fun and creative (see pages 94–96). Each prompt is written in the same three-sentence style. If you choose to write your own prompts, please take a moment to glance at these hints to help you follow the proper format. This will help your students respond to your assignment and will provide extra practice in interpreting prompts.

- Most prompts are written about two grade levels below the reading ability of the students for whom they are intended. If you are writing for fourth graders, you need to use very simple language that even your struggling readers can understand.

- Use standard language in the direction sentence (the third sentence of the prompt). If you want your students to create a narrative, ask them to "tell about," "write about," "write a story," or write about "what happens next." Do not ask them to "explain" what happened next, because *explain* is a word that belongs in the expository prompt.

- Similarly, if you want students to create an expository essay, ask them to "tell how," "tell why," or "explain." Do not ask them to "write a story" if you do not want a narrative.

- Avoid words like *always, never,* and *everyone.* Instead of saying, "Everyone has a best friend," say, "Almost everyone has someone who is special to them." This will make it easier for a child who may not have a best friend.

- Try to keep your prompts positive. Instead of asking students to write about the saddest day of their lives, the person they miss most, or a time they were injured, make sure your prompts are upbeat. Students struggle to write about dark subjects, and the pain can become the focus of the writing rather than the writing lesson at hand. Positive prompts also help students look forward to writing class.

- Keep your prompts rooted in what's real to your students. I was once in a Florida classroom where the teacher asked students to write about a time they played in the snow! This was an impossible assignment for all but three children. Students understandably have difficulty writing about unfamiliar topics or things they've never experienced. Better to have them write about how they spent a rainy day than a day they spent on Mars.

Narrative Writing

Use a giant plus sign to plan your writing.

1 Write the name of the main character in your story. List who else will be in the story. Tell where the story happens.

2 Write what happened first. It may be helpful for you to write what you were doing just before the main action took place.

4 Write how the story ended.

3 Write what happened second. This is usually where the most important action takes place.

Remember! You will begin with box 1 for the introduction and then write about what happened in boxes 2, 3, and 4. You will end back at box 1 because you are writing in a circle.

Expository Writing

Use a giant plus sign to plan your writing.

1 Write the subject of your essay. Tell one interesting thing here.

2 Write reason #1. (If you are telling steps in a process, the first step goes here.)

4 Write reason #3 (or the third step in a process).

3 Write reason #2 (or the second step in the process).

Remember! You will begin with box 1 for the introduction and then write about each of the three reasons listed in boxes 2, 3, and 4. You will end back at box 1 because you are writing in a circle.

Name _____ Date _____

Descriptive Writing

Use a giant plus sign to plan your writing.

1 Write the subject of the paragraph.

2 Write *taste, smell, sound, feel,* and *sight*. Make sure you describe the scene, event, or object using as many of the five senses as possible.

4 Write how the object, event, or scene makes you feel.

3 Write how the object acts, moves, or makes others move or act.

Remember! **Close your paragraph by restating what it is you have been describing.**

Crafting Strong Introductions and Closings

An introduction has two purposes: It should tell the reader what the piece is about and it should make the reader want to read it. But often the hardest part of writing an essay or story is getting started. This chapter will provide you and your students with five fail-proof ways to begin any essay or story.

There are, of course, many ways to begin a piece of writing. If you present students with just these five, they will have essential tools for writing quality introductions. Although many students believe otherwise, an introduction does not tell what happens first in a story. Nor is it the first step in a process or the first "reason why." Look at samples of exemplary writing in your state to determine the length of introduction that your scorers expect.

LESSON 1

Beginning Narratives

Let students know that getting started is often the most difficult part of writing. Assure them that today's lesson will give them skills for beginning any kind of story. We have provided directions for a whole-group lesson. Use the reproducible on page 27 to help with this lesson.

STEP 1

Use chart paper, the chalkboard, or an interactive whiteboard to present this prompt to the class.

➡ *Think about a time you found something. What was it? Write a story about a time you found something interesting.*

■ **USE A SOUND OR MOTION WORD** Tell your class that one way to begin an essay is to use a sound or motion word. Write this on the chalkboard: *Click, click! That is the sound I heard as I was walking down the sidewalk in front of my house.* Point out the comma between the words, the exclamation mark, and how you started a new sentence with a capital letter and ended it with a period. Model your next sentence by writing: *Suddenly I found a penny that I will always cherish.*

See if students can suggest a sound that one might hear if someone was about to find something. Write one or two of their suggestions on the board or

chart paper, then ask them to suggest two follow-up sentences that will tell where the story is about to take place and maybe one hint about the found object.

■ **POSE A QUESTION** Tell your class that a second way to begin a story or an essay is to use a question. Write this on a board or chart paper: *Have you ever found something really interesting?* Point out how you've begun the sentence with a capital letter and ended with a question mark. Once again, you need a second sentence, so now write: *This is the story about a time I found something that changed my life.*

Ask the class if anyone else can think of a way to begin this story with a question. Write their suggestions on the board. Then ask them for a second sentence that might indicate where the object was found or something interesting about the found object.

■ **USE A QUOTATION** Another way to begin an essay is to use a quotation—words spoken by someone—but not a conversation. (See "Writing dialogue" on page 20.) What you want here is just a couple of words or a short sentence. Choose one of these examples: *"Look at that,"* *yelled my brother George. "You won't believe what I found on the sidewalk."* OR *"Find a penny, pick it up, and all the day you'll have good luck." That penny on the sidewalk was the start of a crazy day for me.* Point out the punctuation you have used in the sentence.

■ **START "TALKING"** An easy way to begin a story is to "just start talking." Write this example: *One day I was walking down the sidewalk and found something really interesting. I could hardly believe my eyes!*

Once again, ask the whole group for an alternative "just start talking" sentence and write it on the board or chart paper.

■ **RESTATE THE PROMPT** The fifth way to begin an essay is by doing something that students often do on state writing

Help for struggling and inexperienced writers

Some students will find learning these five techniques to be just too much for one lesson. Make this easier for your more struggling students by dividing your instruction into five mini-lessons. Once you have introduced one of the ways to begin, have small groups of students come up with their own wording and their own introduction. Help build your students' confidence by having them read their group ideas out loud.

If students are *really* struggling, then don't present all five ways. Pick out two or three, and make sure they get good at those. They will only get to showcase one way on the actual state assessment.

A format for teaching

You will notice that many of the lessons in this book follow a similar format: Before making any assignment, present a model, engage the class in a whole-group activity, and assist students with a small-group activity. During these steps, students will work out any questions or misunderstandings they may have, and they will strengthen their own knowledge of the task at hand. While this method of teaching cannot, obviously, be followed on every assignment, try to do it in these writing lessons, and as often as possible with other subjects in your classroom. You will soon find that when your students get to the actual independent work, they approach it with confidence and skill. Without these steps, teachers are not teaching at all; they are simply making assignments.

assessments, especially if they have trouble getting started on their work. They simply restate the prompt. Begin by rereading the prompt. *(Think about a time you found something. What was it? Write a story about a time you found something interesting.)* Then rearrange the words to make an opening sentence. For example: *Everyone has found something. I am going to tell about a time I found an interesting object.*

Once again, ask students how you might begin this essay by using the prompt to help you get started. Write their suggestion on the chalkboard.

STEP 2

Review the five ways to begin an essay. Now have students work in small groups and use the five examples to begin their own narratives about a time they found something (see page 27). Allow about 30 minutes for students to write the five introductions and, if there is time, permit each group to present one or two of its paragraphs to the class.

STEP 3

Present the following prompt:

> ➡ *Everyone has gone for some kind of a ride. Think about a time you rode on something or inside of something. Write a story about a time you went on an exciting ride.*

Have students reread the prompt and then choose one way to begin a story about that ride. Have each child work independently to create an effective paragraph for this kind of prompt.

STEP 4

Circulate around the room to answer any questions and clarify any misconceptions your students may have. Writing this introduction should take about 5–7 minutes.

■ When everyone is finished, ask for a show of hands: How many began with a sound word? A question? A quotation? How many started talking, or restated the prompt? Assure students that all of these are acceptable ways to begin.

■ If time allows, and you think it would be beneficial, have students read these out loud.

 Help for struggling and inexperienced writers

Save the independent work for another day. Begin with a thorough review of the ways to begin and end, and then ask students to try writing an introduction of their own. If necessary, take a vote on the kind of introduction you will use on this day and have each group member write an introduction using that same technique.

LESSON 2

Beginning Expository and Descriptive Essays

As you teach this lesson, point out its similarity to the lesson you just presented on narratives. Use the reproducible on page 28 to help with this lesson.

STEP 1

Use chart paper, the chalkboard, or an interactive whiteboard to present this prompt to the class:

➡ *Everyone has someone who is special to them. Who is special to you? Write an essay to tell why someone is special to you.*

Look carefully at this prompt and point out that it is an expository prompt because it is asking the child to provide information (reasons why something is

 Help for struggling and inexperienced writers

Getting started is the most difficult part of writing. When your students are still learning how to write essays and stories, have them work as a whole group or in small groups to create an introduction that will be used by everyone in the group. Obviously, you will not continue to do this all year long, just until students have grasped the idea of how to get started.

Adaptation for descriptive prompt

Different states have different requirements for writing descriptive prompts. Some states only expect the students to write a paragraph or two; others require a full five-paragraph essay to get a high score. Help your students interpret sample prompts from your state so you can determine the requirements for your students. Then help them with introductions. Remember, the five ways of beginning apply no matter what kind of writing the child is going to do—even persuasive writing can begin in one of these five ways.

true) whereas, in the previous day's prompt, children were asked to tell a story about an experience.

■ Let them know that even though the prompt is asking them to explain, they can still choose to write either fiction or nonfiction—real or pretend reasons that someone is special.

STEP 2

Remind the class that one way to begin an essay is to use a sound or motion word. Write this example for them to read: *Clap, clap! That is what I heard as I entered my living room and saw my best friend, Sylvia, standing there. Sylvia has been my friend for more than five years.*

Ask students if they will help you come up with a way to begin this essay that will use two sound or motion words. Write their suggestions on the board or chart paper.

■ The first two words of the introduction are separated by a comma and end with an exclamation mark.

■ Note that one of the sentences told the reader where the event took place and another told how long the writer had known her friend.

STEP 3

Continue to the second way to begin an essay: with a question. Write this on your board or chart paper: *Do you have a special person who is important to you? I do, and her name is Sylvia. I met Sylvia at a volleyball game, and we have been friends ever since.*

Once again, have your students come up with a question that will serve as an introduction to this essay, along with one or two follow-up sentences. Write their questions and sentences on the board. Point out that you began with a question and added two more sentences to make a short introduction for your essay.

Writing dialogue

Writing conversation is difficult for most elementary school students. They rarely include speech tags, and they have great difficulty with the punctuation.

What are you doing? Nothing. Said Bill. Want to go for some lunch? No, I already ate.

In this example, we cannot tell how many people are in the conversation and who is saying what. Worst of all, the conversations that students add to their writing are often mindless exchanges that simply fill up the page. They do not usually advance the story line or add information. If you read Jenna's sample essays (pages 91–93), you will see that some students can use dialogue effectively and naturally, but your struggling students will fare better if they write in the third person and avoid conversations.

STEP 4

Revisit how to begin with a quotation. Tell your students that a quotation is the exact words that have been said by a person, but in this case, it is simply a one-sentence quotation, not a conversation.

Write this example on the board: *"Happy birthday to you!" That is what my friend Sylvia was singing when I walked in the living room. Sylvia has been my friend for five years, and she has never forgotten my birthday.*

Ask if they can think of another quotation to begin this essay. You may suggest that they use a personal greeting that they might use with a friend ("Anna, Banana!"), or they can think of a more popular greeting to use ("Whassup?"). Be sure to write their suggestions on the board.

■ These serve as models for students as they work in small groups and individually.

■ Point out the quotation marks and commas that punctuate these sentences.

STEP 5

A fourth way to begin an essay is to simply start "talking." In this method, the writer simply begins writing with a couple of statements. Explain this to your students, and then write this example for them. *I have a best friend named Sylvia. She has been my friend ever since I met her at a volleyball game five years ago.*

Following the lesson pattern, now elicit suggestions from the whole group. Write these on the board.

■ This is the easiest way to begin, so they should be able to come up with one or two examples.

How many sentences go into a paragraph?

Avoid giving students a required number of sentences to make a complete paragraph. When we do this, we often see students writing immature, short sentences just to meet the quota. ("It was fun" will appear in 90% of their essays!) Writers are better off with a wonderful one- or two-sentence paragraph than a paragraph with five rudimentary, poorly written sentences.

STEP 6

As in the narratives lesson, the final way to begin an essay is to simply restate the prompt. Encourage students to use this method only if they cannot remember the other four ways, or if nothing clever comes to their minds.

Have your students reread the prompt: *Everyone has someone who is special to them. Who is special to you? Write an essay to tell why someone is special to you.*

Show them one way to rearrange the words to create an introduction. *I have someone who is special to me. I will tell you about my best friend, Sylvia.* Once again, have the students come up with an alternative way to restate this prompt. Write their suggestion on the board as an example.

STEP 7

Review the five ways to begin an essay. Now have students work in small groups and use the five examples to begin their own expository essay about a person who is special to them (see page 28). Allow about 30 minutes for students to write the five introductions and, if there is time, permit each group to present one or two of its paragraphs to the class.

Help for struggling and inexperienced writers

Some students will find learning these five techniques to be just too much for one lesson. Make it easier for these students by dividing your instruction into five mini-lessons. Once you have introduced one of the ways to begin, have small groups of students come up with their own wording and their own introduction. Help build your students' confidence by having them read their group ideas out loud.

If students are *really* struggling, then don't present all five ways. Pick out two or three and make sure they get good at those. They will only get to showcase one way on the actual state assessment.

Group conflicts

When students are working in a group, they often try to outdo, out-funny, or out-gross each other. You need to maintain classroom control, of course, but during this lesson, allow students to have fun. They may decide that they were walking on Mars when they discovered an iPhone in a crater. They may focus on finding a talking Cheerio in their breakfast cereal. As long as they are learning the five ways to begin their essay and they are following the format, encourage their creativity while you warn them that they may be asked to write a whole essay on this topic!

And speaking of group work, even the best-behaved students may have firmly held ideas about what the group should present to the rest of the class. If a child is adamant about what he wants to use and the group has chosen something else, remind the student that he can "hold that thought" and use it when he writes an independent story about this prompt. That way, his work will be unique and will stand out from the rest of the class.

STEP 8

Now present the following prompt:

> ➤ *Almost everyone has a favorite season of the year. Think about what time of year you especially enjoy. Now write an essay to explain why a particular season is your favorite.*

Have students reread the prompt and then choose *one* way to begin an essay about their favorite season. Have each child work independently to create an effective paragraph for this kind of prompt.

Circulate around the room to answer questions or clarify any misconceptions your students may have. Writing this introduction should take about 5–7 minutes.

■ When everyone is finished, ask for a show of hands: How many began with a sound word? A question? A quotation? How many started talking or restated the prompt? Assure them that all of these are acceptable ways to begin.

■ If time allows, and you think it would be beneficial, have students read these out loud.

To list or not to list

Many instructors encourage students to include in the introduction the reasons they are about to explain and to mention these again in the conclusion.

SAMPLE INTRODUCTION: *I have a best friend named Sylvia. She has been my friend ever since I met her at a volleyball game five years ago. Sylvia is special to me because we love to shop, we tell each other secrets, and together we laugh about out little brothers.*

The writer would then write a paragraph each about the three reasons: shopping, secrets, and little brothers, and restate these in the closing paragraph.

SAMPLE CLOSING: *Now you can see why my best friend, Sylvia, is special to me. We love to shop, tell secrets, and laugh about our little brothers. I am glad that Sylvia and I have been friends for five years.*

This is a perfectly acceptable way for students to create a frame for their writing. However, using this format can make the writing seem contrived and uninteresting. The student who writes in this format will probably pass the state assessment, but unless the rest of the writing is outstanding, the score will be just average.

Another problem with listing the three reasons in the introduction is that students think they need to do this with every piece they write. This poses a problem when they try to use this same format for narrative writing. In a narrative, the writer is not expected to provide "reasons why," so students sometimes write the three main events of the story and include these in the introduction. This makes for confused and disjointed writing that will surely get a low score on a state assessment.

RULE OF THUMB: If your students are going to be assessed only on expository writing, you can have them list the reasons in the introduction. If they are going to be assessed on narrative writing only, do not have them use this format, even in expository pieces they do for practice.

 Help for struggling and inexperienced writers

Recommend this listing format to the writers who struggle the most to get words on the page. Having a simple, well-defined format with clear instructions will help these students obtain a passing score.

LESSON 3

How to End an Essay or Story

It is vitally important for young writers to realize that the introduction of an essay is not the first thing that happened in a story or the "first reason why" in an essay. Similarly, the closing is not the last thing that happened in a narrative, nor is it the final reason why in an essay. These two paragraphs should stand out clearly from the rest of the paper, thus demonstrating the writer's organizational skills.

Quality writing is often described as being "whole and complete." This means that the writer has included enough details, examples and/or description to paint a clear picture in the reader's mind. But it is the end of the piece that is the last thing a reader sees, and it is here that a good writer has his or her last chance to make a memorable impression.

One way that student writers can do this is by "writing in a circle." This means simply to choose an idea, phrase, name, scene, or situation from the introduction and use it again in the closing. Some writers may choose to use the exact words from the introduction, while some like to add their own little twist on them. Use the reproducibles on pages 29 and 30 to help with this lesson.

STEP 1

Retrieve the saved charts or documents from your lesson on the ways to begin an essay. Put up the first example and explain that the five ways to end an essay are the same as the five ways to begin.

Here is the example that used sound words in the introduction. *Click, click! That is the sound I heard as I was walking down the sidewalk in front of my house. Suddenly I found a penny that I will always cherish.*

Make sure that students realize that after this introduction there would be three to five paragraphs that tell the story of finding something. After that, the writer is left with the closing.

STEP 2

Write this on the board or chart paper: *I think of that penny often when I am walking on my sidewalk. It was a discarded penny, but now you know why it is a cherished coin.*

Ask students if they can tell you why this is a good ending. They may say that the author took two words from the introduction and reused them in the closing. Circle those: *sidewalk* and *penny.*

■ Explain to your class that by using these same words again, the story seems "whole and complete."

■ It shows the reader that the writer had a definite plan in mind, and it tells the reader that the story is finished—no need to turn the page.

STEP 3

Now put up the next introduction and conduct a mini-lesson in which you ask your students if they can think of a way to use one or two sentences from the following introduction to create an ending.

Have you ever found something really interesting? This is the story about a time I found something that changed my life.

Write their suggestions on the board and discuss which ones are effective. Point out that they may choose to use several words from the introduction or they may use only one or two. (Example: *Clink, clink. That is the sound of that penny going into my bank. That penny changed my life and I will keep it forever!*)

STEP 4

Now it is their turn to create a closing of their own. Put up the third introduction: *"Find a penny, pick it up, and all the day you'll have good luck." That penny on the sidewalk was the start of a crazy day for me.* Remind students that they need to use a phrase, a word, or an idea from this introduction. (If you use the other example, you might also say that they could use a person's name to complete the circle.) Try to have every group read its closing out loud to the class. The more examples the students have, the better they will be at creating their own closings.

STEP 5

Finally, put up the fourth introduction: *One day I was walking down the sidewalk and found something really interesting. I could hardly believe my eyes!* Before they begin writing independently, remind them that there are five ways to begin and there are five ways to end—and they are the same ways!

■ The beauty of this plan is that while the beginning and ending have to have something in common, they do not have to match!

■ Writers are free to start with a sound word and end with a question; they can start with a quote and end by restating the prompt.

Ask students to create a two-sentence closing using something from this introduction. Have students share their ideas with a small group or with the whole class. When they finish, challenge them to write a different closing using a different method.

■ If they ended this one with a question, have them try a quotation.

■ If they ended with simple sentences (in "just start talking") have them write a new closing using sound or motion words.

■ This will prove to them that there is no right or wrong way to write, and that is probably the second most valuable part of this lesson.

You do not need to repeat this with all of the expository essays, but please remind students to use this technique whenever they are writing a story or an essay.

Make sure you copy the chart on page 30 and distribute it to students to keep in their writing folders.

Also copy and distribute the Keys to Good Writing (page 31). This page serves as a great reminder of what was covered in the previous lessons.

 Help for struggling and inexperienced writers

Many writers who struggle are convinced that whatever they do, they are sure they will get it "wrong." This activity provides many variations on an introduction and shows that, if it makes sense, it is "good!" If your students are struggling, be sure to repeat this activity with the expository introductions or with another prompt. For those who are still confused by the lesson, have these students match the introduction to the closing every time. If they began with a question, they should end with a question. If they began with a quote, they should end with a quote. Simplifying the format enables these students to make one decision fewer and increases their chances of writing a cohesive essay.

Five Ways to Begin a Narrative Essay

Read the prompt. Then read each of the five ways to begin a narrative essay. After each example, write your own introduction for this narrative.

Prompt ➡ Think about a time you found something. What was it? Write a story about a time you found something interesting.

How to Begin	Example	Write Your Own
1. Use a sound or motion word. Include up to two more sentences.	*Click, click! That is the sound I heard as I was walking down the sidewalk in front of my house. Suddenly I found a penny that I will always cherish.*	
2. Pose a question. Include up to two more sentences.	*Have you ever found something really interesting? This is the story about a time I found something that changed my life.*	
3. Use a quotation. Include up to two more sentences.	*"Look at that," yelled my brother George. "You won't believe what I found on the sidewalk." OR "Find a penny, pick it up and all the day you'll have good luck." That penny on the sidewalk was the start of a crazy day for me.*	
4. Start "talking."	*One day I was walking down the sidewalk and found something really interesting. I could hardly believe my eyes!*	
5. Restate the prompt. Rearrange the words in the prompt to create an opening paragraph.	*Everyone has found something. I am going to tell about a time I found an interesting object.*	

Five Ways to Begin an Expository or Descriptive Essay

Read the prompt. Then read each of the five ways to begin an expository essay. After each example, write your own introduction.

Prompt ➔ Everyone has someone who is special to them. Who is special to you? Write an essay to tell why someone is special to you.

How to Begin	Example	Write Your Own
1. Use a sound or motion word. Include up to two more sentences	*Clap, clap! That is what I heard as I entered my living room and saw my best friend, Sylvia, standing there. Sylvia has been my friend for more than five years.*	
2. Pose a question. Include up to two more sentences.	*Do you have a special person who is important to you? I do, and her name is Sylvia. I met Sylvia at a volleyball game, and we have been friends ever since.*	
3. Use a quotation. Include up to two more sentences.	*"Happy birthday to you!" That is what my friend Sylvia was singing when I walked in the living room. Sylvia has been my friend for five years, and she has never forgotten my birthday.*	
4. Start "talking."	*I have a best friend named Sylvia. She has been my friend ever since I met her at a volleyball game five years ago.*	
5. Restate the prompt. Rearrange the words in the prompt to create an opening paragraph.	*I have someone who is special to me. I will tell you about my best friend, Sylvia.*	

Five Ways to End an Essay or Story

An effective way to end an essay or story is to choose words from the introduction and use them in the closing. We call this "writing in a circle."

Read the first introduction and the sample closing. Then write your own closing for each introduction.

Introduction	Closing
Click, click! That is the sound I heard as I was walking down the sidewalk in front of my house. Suddenly I found a penny that I will always cherish.	I think of that penny often when I am walking on my sidewalk. It was a discarded penny, but now you know why it is a cherished coin.
Have you ever found something really interesting? This is the story about a time I found something that changed my life.	
"Find a penny, pick it up, and all the day you'll have good luck." That penny on the sidewalk was the start of a crazy day for me.	
One day I was walking down the sidewalk and found something really interesting. I could hardly believe my eyes!	
Everyone has found something. I am going to tell about a time I found an interesting object.	

Five Ways to Begin and End Your Work

There are five good ways to begin and end a piece of writing.

In the chart below, write an example of each of the five ways.

Five Ways to Begin and End	Introduction Example	Closing Example
USE A SOUND OR MOTION WORD		
POSE A QUESTION		
USE A QUOTATION		
START TALKING		
RESTATE THE PROMPT		

Keys to Good Writing

 READ THE PROMPT AT LEAST TWO TIMES. Take a minute to think about the prompt. Look for clue words. Decide if the clues tell you to write a narrative, expository, or descriptive piece.

- Narrative prompts expect you to tell a story. They will have the clue words "write about," "tell about," "what happened next?" or "write a story about." Remember that the story can be real (nonfiction) or pretend (fiction), but it needs to be about *you*.

- Expository prompts expect you to explain something. They will have the clue words "tell why," "tell how," or "explain." Remember that your essay can be real (nonfiction) or pretend (fiction).

- Descriptive prompts expect you to describe something—more than just what it looks like. They will have the clue words "tell about" or "describe." Remember that you can describe action, a scene, thoughts, moods, or emotions.

 MAKE A PLAN FOR WRITING. Choose an easy, logical graphic organizer, such as a page divided into quarters. Reserve one area for any notes about your introduction and closing. Use the other three areas to plan the body of the essay. This is where you will jot notes about key events, reasons or supporting details, steps in a process, and so on.

 THINK ABOUT THE FIVE WAYS TO BEGIN AND END.

- Use sound or motion words. Sound: *Snip, snip! That is the sound I heard the day my little sister cut off my hair!* Motion: *Twist, twist! That is what I kept doing to my loose tooth.*

- Pose a question. *Do you have someone who is special to you?*

- Use a quotation. *"There's no place like home."*

- Start talking. *One day I was walking in the hallway at school and something very unusual happened to me.*

- Restate the prompt. *Almost everyone has a favorite day of the week. I will tell you why I love Fridays.*

 CRAFT A STRONG INTRODUCTION AND CLOSING. Each one will have at least two or three sentences. Select from the five ways to begin and end. You can begin your essay with a quotation and end it with a question. Or, you can begin by restating the prompt and end with a quotation. Any combination is acceptable. Remember to "write in a circle," by choosing a word, an idea, a phrase, or a name from the introduction and reuse it in the closing.

CHAPTER 3

Moving Beyond the Basics

Because writing is often a neglected subject, many, many students arrive in the fourth or fifth grade with no idea of how to write an essay or how to narrate a story. You have to begin somewhere, and the five-paragraph narrative is the best and easiest place to start. It is not, however, where we want our writing instruction to end! This chapter will begin with the basics and then demonstrate easy ways to get beyond the five-paragraph format and into more complex, sophisticated writing.

Pros, cons, and suggestions for using the five-paragraph essay:

In recent years there has been a great deal of discussion about the best format for beginning or struggling writers. Because it is easy to use and will usually get students a passing score on state writing assessments, teaching students to write five-paragraph essays or stories is the preferred method among most elementary school teachers. Here are some pros and cons of teaching this kind of writing.

PRO This format is excellent to use on state standardized writing assessments. Because students usually have only 45 minutes in which to plan and create a piece of writing, this simple format provides them with an effective and time-efficient tool.

CON Teaching *only* the five-paragraph essay will limit your students' writing. They will think that five paragraphs make a complete story, and that is rarely true.

Suggestion: If your students will be taking a state assessment in writing, by all means teach the lessons in this book using this format. Have students continue to build on these skills by adding paragraphs to describe the character's thoughts, the action, and further descriptions of the scenes. Students can add additional events to their stories. In expository writing, they can provide examples and vignettes to support their points. Teach the five-paragraph as a skeleton on which students can build longer, more in-depth pieces.

 Help for struggling and inexperienced writers

This chapter contains several write-your-own-essay reproducible pages. If you are dealing with struggling or inexperienced writers, they are quite likely to be struggling readers, too. If this is the case, go through these pages very slowly and treat them like an instructional lesson, not an assignment. Depending on the needs of your class, read the words in italics on the Writing Activity pages out loud and pause to explain or offer more suggestions as you go along. It may also help to keep the class together as you complete these pages.

Teachers often work quickly to get students to "the next level," so that after they have completed a simple story like the little door story (see Lesson 4), they jump immediately to the next level of difficulty. This is a mistake, especially for the struggling and inexperienced writers. Allow students the opportunity to practice what they have learned before moving on to harder assignments. When you have the patience to do this, you will find that students have actually grasped the concepts and mastered the skills, which will make moving to the next level much easier and will keep you from having to do so much reteaching. If your students wrote to the little door prompt, until they gain confidence, have them write a second and third narrative essay using the same format and transition phrases. Before you know it, there will be far more than two extension sentences, and you will be ready for the next step in the writing process.

Quality instruction is not a speedy process. If students have arrived in your classroom with limited writing skills, it may take a week to complete an activity such as writing the little door story. Take the whole week and provide your best instruction every step of the way. You can follow the same pattern in subsequent essays, but each one will take a little less time. Eventually students should be able to respond to a prompt within the time allotted by the state.

PRO The five-paragraph essay or story is easily lengthened with descriptions, examples, and elaborations that will assure the student of a high score on a state assessment, not just a passing score.

CON The five-paragraph essay can be very limiting to the more creative, capable writers. It can also encourage students to write stiff, contrived pieces that lack personality and interest.

Suggestion: Use your professional judgment and thoroughly assess your students' writing abilities, the time you have in your schedule for writing, and the requirements of your state writing assessment. What does your state consider to be exemplary writing? You can probably find examples on the Web site of your state's department of education. Work hard to get every child to the level that your state considers exemplary, but do not expect every child to write the same length or style of essay—especially if you have students who are naturally gifted in writing.

One more thing: State writing assessments are typically administered in the early spring. That still leaves one-fourth of the school year during which you can have students try out all kinds of writing: book reports, poetry, creative nonfiction, free writing, and various genres, such as science fiction and mystery. Just because the test is over, don't stop teaching writing and don't stop building on the wonderful base of writing skills that you have worked so hard on during the school year.

LESSON 4

Narrative Essays

Begin with Rashad's story about a time he went through a little door. His is a very simple story, but it does contain an introduction with a quotation, three paragraphs in the body, and it is written in a circle. In most states this essay would receive a middle score (2 on a scale of 1–4; 3 on a scale of 1–6). Here is how to replicate this lesson in your own classroom. Use the reproducibles on pages 44–46 to help with this lesson.

STEP 1

Pass out copies of the Narrative Prompt and graphic organizer on page 44. Have students begin by reading the prompt and scaffolded questions on the graphic organizer.

STEP 2

Pass out copies of Rashad's story (page 45). Students should read the story and complete the activity on the page.

Answers: 1. Line under "A Little Door." 2. Circle around "Please take these papers to the office." 3. Stars over "While I was," "I peeked," and "I decided" 4. Lines under "While I was walking, I decided to get a drink of water." "I peeked at it and decided to go in." "I decided to duck right back out, but the door was gone!" 5. Squares around "Mrs. Blake" and "papers"

 Help for struggling and inexperienced writers

Circulate as students are writing and check for progress. Carry some tiny stickers or a marker, and when you see students who are on the right track, put a little smiley face, star, or sticker at the top of their worksheet. This will build the child's confidence and help him or her keep going to the end of the story. This is far better than not looking at the paper until it is finished, only to realize that the child was on the wrong track.

STEP 3

Next, students should reread the prompt and fill in the Introduction quadrant of the graphic organizer. This is a perfect opportunity to model how to use this graphic organizer format by filling it in as Rashad may have.

STEP 4

After everyone has completed the introduction, have them continue to the second quadrant. Beginning the next sentence with "I was just…," "While I was…," or "When I was…," they should write what they were doing *before* the main event, followed by two more sentences that give more information about that particular activity.

■ What students are actually doing here is establishing the setting and introducing the characters. You cannot, however, just tell them to do that, so you provide or suggest a way to begin the story part of the essay.

■ The idea of telling what was going on before the main event in the story is a good one. Professional authors sometimes take several chapters to do this.

STEP 5

After the setting is established and the characters have been introduced (even in just two or three sentences), it is time to move to the third quadrant. This focuses on the main event. Your students can begin with any one of several transition words or phrases. Help them write at least three sentences to tell about going through the door and what they saw and did.

■ You may need to encourage them to write more. Try asking questions that elicit detailed responses. *Were there any people in the room? Did you eat anything? Did you talk to anyone?*

STEP 6

Once there are enough details about the main event, it's time to move to the fourth quadrant to begin wrapping up the writing. "I decided…" is a great transition phrase because it can connect to almost anything. Rashad uses it here so that he can easily return to the classroom. In this case, it is one way to end the story quickly—a real help when the assessment has a time limit.

STEP 7

Remind students to close by writing in a circle. They should revisit the first quadrant to help them conclude their piece.

 Help for struggling and inexperienced writers

Some students tend to make their stories far too complicated. *(I woke up in the morning and went to school. It was locked. I ended up on Mars. Then I was the king. I lived in a castle. Then I was not the king anymore.)*

■ Help students write a complete story by insisting that the story take place on one day, in one time, and in one place. This will simplify the story by limiting the number of events, allowing the student to concentrate on adding the kind of descriptive details that make writing interesting.

Other students tell the whole story in the introduction sentence. *(This is a story about a time I put on cowboy boots and rode a big horse and fell off and broke my arm.)* Of course, this is not a complete story, and it would probably be scored at level 1 in most states.

■ Instead of having this child rewrite his introduction, have the next sentence begin with "It all began when…" This will give the child a chance to redeem himself by writing one paragraph to explain where the story took place and who else was there, one about the actual ride, and one about how he fell off and broke his arm.

Personal narrative

Almost every state that requires students to write to a narrative prompt asks the child to create a "personal narrative." This means writing a story in the first person. The event can be true or imaginary, but it must involve the writer. Students should not be writing about another person's experience.

STEP 8

Pass out copies of page 46. Students will apply what they have learned by writing to a new prompt. For additional practice, this lesson can be used with almost every prompt that is listed in our bank of narrative prompts found on page 94.

Guide students by helping them in much the same way you did with this lesson. Do not assume that because you helped them with the one or two essays that they are ready to work as independent writers. Try giving several narrative essays, using the same pattern each and every time, and following a "gradual release" philosophy, where each time they do this activity you help them less and less but expect more and more independence and quality writing.

LESSON 5

Enhancing Narrative Essays

Beginning writers learn two basic ways to add an elaboration to a narrative. They can add conversation or they can add full paragraphs of description. It is usually difficult for children to write effective dialogue, so we will stick to adding description paragraphs.

Generally speaking, when students include a whole separate paragraph of description, it will raise their state assessment writing score by one whole point. By including two or more such paragraphs, students can raise their score by as much as two points. This is, of course, assuming that the description uses some type of figurative language and/or strong verbs, adjectives, and adverbs.

When we ask students to describe, they usually use their five senses and write a description consisting largely of sensory characteristics. But there is a lot more to description than just that. We want students to describe thoughts, the mood, a scene, and action. Use the reproducibles on pages 47 and 48 to help with this lesson.

STEP 1

If you had your students write to the little door prompt (page 44), have them retrieve it from their writing folders and reread it.

Test tip

Including a whole separate paragraph of description will raise a student's state assessment writing score by one whole point. Two or more such paragraphs can raise a score by as much as two points.

STEP 2

Once all students have a pair of scissors and access to some transparent tape, have them cut the story apart just after the second paragraph. Have them tape one half-sheet of paper between the second paragraph and the rest of the story. On this half-sheet, have them describe the door in detail. Ask them to tell what it is made of, what color it is, if it has windows, a doorknob, a sign, hinges, and any other details they can think of.

STEP 3

Now have them make a second cut after the third paragraph. Once again, they should tape a half-sheet of paper between the end of the paragraph and the rest of the story in order to add another description, providing more details about the scene. In Rashad's example, this is where he more completely described the scene in the teacher's lounge.

STEP 4

Finally, have them cut a third half-sheet and tape it after the fourth paragraph. This time, you should instruct them to either describe action or their thoughts.

STEP 5

Pass out copies of Rashad's story *with* the elaborations (page 47). Be sure to read it aloud while students follow along. I am sure you will agree that it is now a much more effective essay. Then, students will apply what they have learned by writing to a new prompt (page 48).

LESSON 6

Expository Essays

In an expository essay, the writer gives reasons why, explains, or tells the steps in a process. On expository essays, students often fail to include enough information to earn a high score. This lesson is intended to help you help your students create a basic five-paragraph essay containing sufficient information to pass a state writing examination. Use the reproducibles on pages 49–51 to help with this lesson.

Pushing the pause button

One easy way to help students include a descriptive paragraph is to ask them to "hit the pause button." They are familiar with this term, of course, because they all know how to use a television remote. For our purposes, hitting the pause button means the moment when we want students to stop telling their story and insert a paragraph describing the scene, some physical characteristics, the character's thoughts, or action. This is exactly what they have done in these activities.

STEP 1

Pass out copies of the Expository Prompt and graphic organizer on page 49. Have students begin by reading the prompt and scaffolded questions on the graphic organizer.

STEP 2

Pass out copies of Tommy's essay (page 50). Students should read the essay and complete the activity on the page.

Answers: 1. Circle around "Phil Hill" and "racecar driver" 2. Lines under "The first reason I would like to meet Phil Hill is that he was the first and only American to win a Formula One World Championship." "The second reason I would like to meet Phil Hill is he raced for Ford Motor Company." "The third reason I would like to meet Phil Hill is that he really liked old cars." 3. Stars over "famous" and "NASCAR" 4. Squares around "The first reason," "The second reason," and "The third reason"; Answers will vary.

STEP 3

Help students fill out the graphic organizer. Emphasize that each of the reasons the organizer asks them to list will become a separate paragraph when they begin writing. It is often difficult for students to complete these organizers because they want to write the whole essay on this page. Encourage them to write in incomplete sentences and to jot down a few notes about what they want to say. If you model doing this, it will be helpful for them.

■ Filling in the graphic organizer first makes it easy to turn the ideas into an essay. Help students with the introduction by using one of the five ways to begin an essay. If it is early in the school year, you should choose one way to begin and have the whole class use it. If your students are accomplished writers, or if they have already had experience with different kinds of introductions, allow them to write this paragraph independently.

■ Because this is an instructional activity, not just an assignment, it is important that you teach this lesson to the whole group.

How to listen to an essay

Most states have benchmarks and standards stating that teachers should give students opportunities to present work orally and that students should also learn listening skills. Most teachers are so busy teaching everything else that these areas are overlooked. Help students with both of these standards by having them read their work out loud as often as you can. This builds confidence, gives students a chance to hear what others are doing, and will reinforce their ideas of what good writing is and what is expected in class.

While you should encourage students to read their work out loud to the class, do not insist that they do it. Your insistence may create more problems than it solves. If a child does not want to read his work out loud, ask if it is OK if you read it out loud instead. If he says yes, read it with great enthusiasm, and let the class see what good work the child has created. If he says he does not want his work read out loud, then respect that and let it go. Even the most insecure writers will eventually allow you to present their work, or even read it out loud themselves, once you have established some ground rules for showing respect to writers.

One more thing—having everyone read out loud takes a long time. If time is an issue for you, have students share their stories with each other in small groups or have them read their work to students from another class of their peers or to younger students in the school.

STEP 4

The second paragraph could begin with "The first reason why I want to meet ____ is ____ ." Then students should add at least two sentences of supporting details to further explain why they want to meet this person.

■ Remind students that they are allowed to be creative in determining the reasons for wanting to meet this person. What you are looking for here is their writing ability and the inclusion of supporting details, not veracity.

STEP 5

The second and third paragraphs should parallel the first: use the reason why as a topic sentence and add two more supporting details. Take a minute to brainstorm other ways of beginning these two paragraphs so that the text will not be so repetitive. For example, "Another reason...," "The last reason...," "Finally...," "I also want to...," "If I met ____ I could...," and "I think..."

STEP 6

After students have given their reasons and explanations, help them write in a circle to create the closing.

STEP 7

Pass out copies of page 51. Students will apply what they have learned by writing to a new prompt.

For additional practice, this lesson format can be used with almost every prompt listed in our bank of expository prompts found on page 95. Guide your students by helping them read and interpret the prompt, create a simple and quick graphic organizer, and write an introduction using one of the five ways to begin an essay.

LESSON 7

Enhancing Expository Essays

If students include an elaboration paragraph in a story or an essay on a state writing assessment, their score usually jumps one or two points, so it is vitally important that you teach your students to include these paragraphs. But students will not always be writing for an assessment. Good writing always requires details, description, examples, and/or vignettes to make them interesting, informative, and complete. Students need to learn to include these paragraphs so that they will become effective writers, period. Use the reproducibles on pages 52 and 53 to help with this lesson.

STEP 1

Distribute copies of page 52. Read aloud Tommy's essay and point out the words in bold. Most will agree that these changes drastically improve his original work.

STEP 2

Next, have students revisit the activity on page 51 and help them insert these elaborations. Students should cut their essays apart after the end of the second paragraph. Here they need to tape one half-sheet of paper between the second paragraph and the rest of the essay. Have them do similar cutting and taping after the third and fourth paragraphs so that each child has a long essay with three blank spaces.

STEP 3

The elaboration paragraph in an expository essay can take several forms. Sometimes authors explain a particular point, write a short vignette, or provide data or other supporting details for their ideas. You can best assist students by sharing some basic transition phrases for these elaboration paragraphs.

STEP 4

Direct students to the first blank space and write the following words on the board or chart paper: *For example*, *The best*, *One time*, *I remember*, *Last*, *Whenever*. Have them choose one of these transition phrases and write a whole paragraph that further supports the ideas in the previous paragraph. Repeat this for the other two blank spaces.

This lesson may take as long as two writing periods. Be patient. This is an instructional lesson, not an assignment.

STEP 5

Distribute copies of page 53. Students will apply what they have learned by writing to a new prompt.

LESSON 8

Descriptive Essays

Description is not a distinct mode of writing, like expository, narrative, and persuasive, but the ability to write descriptively is essential to a host of writing genres. Many state assessments ask students to write essays in which they describe physical characteristics, mood, thoughts, emotions, scenes, and action. Usually when we ask students to describe something, they focus on how it looks. In descriptive writing, we want them to incorporate all of their senses when they describe a setting, the action in a situation, or how it felt to be there. Use the reproducibles on pages 54–56 to help with this lesson.

STEP 1

Pass out copies of the Descriptive Prompt and graphic organizer on page 54. Have students begin by the reading prompt and scaffolded questions on the graphic organizer.

 Help for struggling and inexperienced writers

Most expository essays will ask students to give reasons why, so beginning writers tend to begin every expository paragraph the same way: *The first reason why, the second reason why, the third reason why.*

Point out that while this is a correct response to the prompt, it is boring. Guide students in their writing so that they use "the ___ reason why" only once in an essay. Other times, they can use these paragraph starters: "One reason is that…," "Another reason…," I also think…," "First of all…", "Secondly…," "Last of all…," or "Finally…"

There are a variety of transition phrases students can use on page 59.

However, if you have students who are *really* struggling with writing, do not give them these choices of transition phrases. For this lesson, you should select each of the transitions to begin the next paragraphs—at least this first time. Later, they will be able to self-select and write independently.

Using sentence fragments

While we want our students to write in complete sentences, it is acceptable for them to include sentence fragments, especially if they are used purposefully and to make a point. A good example of this is in Gil's story when he wrote, "Embarrassing? You bet!" This is often a sign of a mature writer and can be a very effective writing element.

STEP 2

Pass out copies of Gil's essay (page 55). Students should read the essay and complete the activity on the page.

Answers: 1. Square around "EPCOT" 2. Lines under "The best place in EPCOT is Spaceship Earth." "The outside of Spaceship Earth is beautiful." "Inside the spaceship everyone rides in little blue cars." 3. Stars over "Disney World" and "EPCOT" 4. Circle around "only babies like that place," "you can tell they are really fake," "Spaceship Earth is the most exciting part"

STEP 3

Next, have students complete the introduction and use the next paragraph to provide a physical description of the whole place, or, like Gil's example, just one part of a place. Help them decide what to describe by providing this list of words: *size, shape, color, smell, action, use, sound, age, texture, taste, movement*

STEP 4

In the next paragraph, students should describe some action that might happen at this place.

■ Nothing exciting going on? Remind students that the essay does not have to be 100% true. It can be about a real place, but what happens there might be fiction.

STEP 5

In the final paragraph, the child should describe how the place makes him or her feel. This will be the most difficult type of description if the child is writing about a place he has never actually visited. Once again, the feelings do not have to be literally true. Provide this list to get your class started: *mood, emotion, feeling, action, thoughts, fears, hopes, opinion.*

■ Remind students to close by writing in a circle.

STEP 6

Pass out copies of page 56. Students will apply what they have learned by writing to a new prompt.

For additional practice, this lesson format can be used with almost every prompt listed in the bank of descriptive prompts found on page 96.

Elaborations as a new paragraph?

Students often ask if the elaboration should be a new paragraph or part of the paragraph that contains the topic sentence and extension. The short answer is: either way is correct. If the elaboration is going to be a long one, then make it a separate paragraph. If the elaboration is three or four sentences, it does not need to be a separate paragraph. The good news: this is not an issue that will help or hurt a score on a state writing assessment.

LESSON 9

Enhancing Descriptive Essays

Gil's essay about Spaceship Earth contained all of the basic elements that have been discussed in this book: introduction and closing, topic sentences followed by extensions. So it was already an excellent descriptive essay. But to move it to the next higher level, he needed to add even more description, perhaps about what happened one time when he was on this ride, information about something he learned, or a paragraph about what someone felt or said. Use the reproducibles on pages 57 and 58 to help with this lesson.

STEP 1

If your students completed the activity on page 56 about an object that was special to them, simply have them cut the essay apart just after the second, third, and fourth paragraphs, tape one half-sheet of blank paper between each of the paragraphs, assembling the essay into one long piece.

■ It is on these blanks that the students will write a more detailed description that will be sure to improve their work and give it a higher score on a state assessment.

STEP 2

Help students by reviewing with them the version of Gil's story about Disney World that includes elaboration (page 57). Gil has described how the park looked at night and what happened when he rode with his little sister. You might suggest to students that they write about what they had to eat, some photographs they took, information about a parade or special sight, or a vignette about a special activity they did.

STEP 3

Pass out copies of page 58. Students will apply what they have learned by writing to a new prompt.

Narrative Prompt

Prompt ➜ You are walking down the hallway of your school and you see a small door. You stoop down and go through it. Write a story about what happens next.

Introduction (and closing)

Who is your teacher? What is happening in your classroom?

Before

What were you doing when you noticed the door? Why were you in the hallway?

End of the story

How do you get back through the door? What happened when you returned to class?

The adventure

This is the main part of the story. What did you see when you went through the door? What action was taking place? What were you thinking? What did you do?

Narrative Essay Activity
(no elaboration)

Look at Rashad's story about the time he found a little door. Use a green crayon, marker, or colored pencil to mark the following elements of his story.

1. Underline the title.

2. Circle the quotation in his introduction.

3. Draw a star above the transition words that begin each paragraph in the body of the story.

4. Underline the three topic sentences in the body of his story.

5. Draw a square around the words that are the same in the introduction and the closing.

"A Little Door" by Rashad

"Please take these papers to the office," said my teacher, Mrs. Blake. I picked up the papers and started out the classroom door. I love it when I get to be the errand runner.

While I was walking, I decided to get a drink of water. When I bent down to the fountain, I noticed a small door. I had never seen it before. I was a little surprised to see it.

I peeked at it and decided to go in. When I got there, I was in for a big surprise. I was in the teacher's lounge! All of the teachers were in there grading papers and drinking Cokes. They were laughing at the funny things that kids do in school.

I decided to duck right back out, but the door was gone! I searched around the teacher's lounge until Mr. Rowland asked me why I was in there. I told him I was lost on the way to the office. His face told me that he did not believe me, but he took me back out into the hallway and I took the papers to the office.

When I got back to Mrs. Blake's room, she asked me how I returned so fast. I had only left 30 seconds ago. She even called the office to make sure the papers had been delivered. You won't believe me, but that door was a time warp!

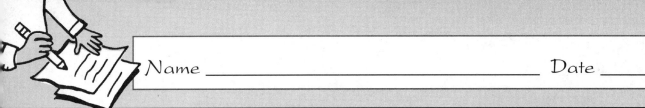

Narrative Prompt and Writing Activity

(no elaboration)

Read the prompt. Then imagine that the words in italics are the words your teacher is saying to you. Write your essay on a separate sheet of paper. Include at least 15 sentences!

Prompt ➡ One day your teacher puts a small box on her desk and leaves the room. A sound comes from the box. Write a story about what happens next.

Introduction: *Think of two sound or motion words you can use to begin your essay. Then write at least two more sentences to complete the introduction. For example:*

_____ ! _____ ! That is what I kept hearing in school today. _____

Body: *Start with, "I was just . . ." This is where you tell what you were doing BEFORE the teacher put the box on her desk and left. Add two more sentences to better explain what was going on in the room.*

Body: *Write about the main event.* Then . . . *Tell what happened when the box made a sound. What kind of sound was it? Did the box move? What did the children say or do? What did you say or do? What was making the sound? Make sure you have at least three sentences in this paragraph.*

Body: *This is the end of the story, so you know the teacher is coming back. What does she see? What does she say? What else did you do or say? Make sure you have at least three sentences in this paragraph.*

Closing: *You need to write in a circle, so go back and reread your introduction. Then write two or three sentences as a closing. Make sure you use at least one word from the introduction here in your closing.*

Narrative Essay Activity
(with elaboration)

"A Little Door" by Rashad

"Please take these papers to the office," said my teacher, Mrs. Blake. I picked up the papers and started out the classroom door. I love it when I get to be the errand runner.

While I was walking, I decided to get a drink of water. When I bent down to the fountain, I noticed a small door. I had never seen it before. I was a little surprised to see it.

The door was made of wood and painted green. It had a little triangle window and a golden doorknob, but no keyhole. It was old and ragged, like an old log. On the front of it was a sign that said, "Kids Keep Out," so I thought it was a place I would like to visit!

The first elaboration is a physical description of the door.

I peeked at it and decided to go in. When I got there, I was in for a big surprise. I was in the teacher's lounge! All of the teachers were in there grading papers and drinking Cokes. They were laughing at the funny things that kids do in school.

The walls were covered with posters saying how great our school was. There were papers and candy on all of the tables. One wall had two soda machines and two candy and snack machines! It was like heaven in there.

The second elaboration is a description of a scene.

I decided to duck right back out, but the door was gone! I searched around the teacher's lounge until Mr. Rowland asked me why I was in there. I told him I was lost on the way to the office. His face told me that he did not believe me, but he took me back out into the hallway and I took the papers to the office.

Now I knew I was in trouble. I thought to myself, Mrs. Blake will yell at me when I finally get back. The kids will probably laugh at me! What will she tell my mom?

The third elaboration is a description of what he was thinking.

When I got back to Mrs. Blake's room, she asked me how I returned so fast. I had only left 30 seconds ago. She even called the office to make sure the papers had been delivered. You won't believe me, but that door was a time warp!

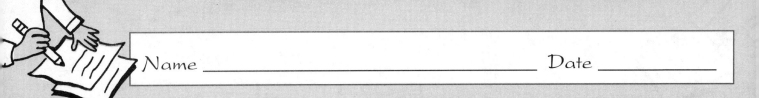

Narrative Prompt and Writing Activity

(with elaboration)

Read the prompt. Then pretend that the words in italics are the words your teacher is saying to you. Write your essay on a separate sheet of paper. Include at least 15 sentences!

Prompt ➡ Have you ever found something interesting? Think about a time you found something. Write a story about a time you found an interesting object.

Introduction: *Think of two sound or motion words you can use to begin your essay. Then write at least two more sentences to complete the introduction. You can tell where you were or whom you were with.*

Body: *Start with, "I was just . . ." and tell what you were doing BEFORE you found the object. Make sure that the last sentence in this paragraph tells what you found!*

Elaboration: *Hit the "pause button"! Write at least three sentences to describe the object that you found. You can tell about the size, the shape, the color, the smell, a noise it makes, whether any writing is on it, how it moves, or any other details.*

Body: *Now tell about what happened as you found it. Be sure to use some action words to tell YOUR action, the action of the object, or the action of someone else in your story. This should be the longest paragraph in the story.*

Elaboration: *Hit the "pause button" again! This time you need to describe your thoughts about the whole situation. It is sort of like you stopped telling the story for a moment to allow the reader to look inside your head and know how you felt. For example:* I thought to myself . . .

Body: *Now you need to end your story. Tell about what happened after you found it. You need three more sentences here. For example:* At last . . .

Closing: *Now end your story by writing in a circle. Make sure you have at least one word from the introduction in the closing.*

Expository Prompt

Prompt ➡ Most kids have someone they admire and would like to meet. Think about someone famous you would like to meet. Write an essay to explain why you would like to meet a certain famous person.

Introduction (and closing)

Tell whom you would like to meet. Tell why that person is famous.

First reason why

Tell one reason you would like to meet this person.

Third reason why

Tell a third reason you would like to meet this person.

Second reason why

Tell a second reason you would like to meet this person.

Expository Essay Activity
(no elaboration)

Look at Tommy's essay about a why he would like to meet a famous person. Use a red crayon, marker, or colored pencil to mark the following elements of this essay.

1. In the introduction, circle the name of the famous person and the reason that person is famous.

2. Underline each of the three topic sentences in the body of the essay.

3. Draw a star over the words that are the same in the introduction and the closing.

4. Draw a square around the transition words that begin each paragraph of the body.

What do you notice about these transitions? _____

Write three different ways Tommy could have begun these sentences.

_____ _____ _____

Phil Hill, Racecar Driver by Tommy

Can you name a famous racecar driver? Most kids will think of Richard Petty or Jimmy Johnson from NASCAR. The driver I would most like to meet is Phil Hill. I won't ever get to meet him because he died in 2008, but if I COULD have met him, here are the reasons why.

The first reason I would like to meet Phil Hill is that he was the first and only American to win a Formula One World Championship. He got to drive great cars like Jaguars, Maseratis, and Ferraris. He won the World Championship in 1961 in a Ferrari.

The second reason I would like to meet Phil Hill is he raced for Ford Motor Company. My dad works for Ford, so I think they are the best cars.

The third reason I would like to meet Phil Hill is that he really liked old cars. He used to write for a magazine and told people how to fix up their cars. Then he was on television talking about cars and he was a judge for famous cars shows.

I won't ever get to meet Phil Hill, but that is the most famous person I would have liked to meet. I still think he was more important than the NASCAR guys.

Expository Prompt and Writing Activity

(no elaboration)

Read the prompt. Then imagine that the words in italics are the words your teacher is saying to you. Write your essay on a separate sheet of paper. Include at least 15 sentences!

Prompt ➜ Everyone has a place they would like to visit. Think about somewhere you have always wanted to go. Now write an essay to tell why you would like to go to a particular place.

Introduction: *Think of a question you could use to begin your essay. Write it first. Then write two more sentences. Be sure you list the name of the place you would like to go and with whom you would like to travel. Tell where it is (for example, what country or state it is in).*

Body: *Finish this sentence:* The first reason I want to go to _____ is . . . *Then write at least two more sentences to explain why you chose this place. If you are stuck, try writing about what you might see at this special place.*

Body: *Finish this sentence:* Another reason to go to _____ is . . . *Then write at least two more sentences to explain a reason you want to visit this place. If you are stuck, write about an activity you could do there.*

Body: *Finish this sentence:* The last reason I want to go to _____ is . . . *Then write at least two more sentences to tell the last reason you have chosen this place. If you are stuck, write about the kinds of foods you might eat while you are visiting this place.*

Closing: *Reread your introduction. Write a closing that includes at least one thing that you used in your introduction. You can use a question, a quotation, a sound word, or just simple sentences to end your essay.*

Expository Essay Activity
(with elaboration)

Phil Hill, Racecar Driver by Tommy

Can you name a famous racecar driver? Most kids will think of Richard Petty or Jimmy Johnson from NASCAR. The driver I would most like to meet is Phil Hill. I won't ever get to meet him because he died in 2008, but if I COULD have met him, here are the reasons why.

The first reason I would like to meet Phil Hill is that he was the first and only American to win a Formula One World Championship. He got to drive great cars like Jaguars, Maseratis, and Ferraris. He won the World Championship in 1961 in a Ferrari.

In the first elaboration, the writer explains how Formula One cars are special.

In case you don't know, Formula One cars are the fastest in the world. They have open wheels and go almost 200 miles an hour. They also don't just go in circles—they go on tracks with lots of sharp curves. The cars look like real racecars, not like the kinds of cars we drive.

The second reason I would like to meet Phil Hill is he raced for Ford Motor Company. My dad works for Ford, so I think they are the best cars.

In the second elaboration, he simply tells more about why he thinks the Ford GT40 is the best car ever created.

My favorite ford is the GT40. It is supposed to be one of the best all-time racing cars. It won the 24 Hours of LeMans four times and it is the only American car to ever win it. I don't think Phil Hill won that race, but I bet he could have!

The third reason I would like to meet Phil Hill is that he really liked old cars. He used to write for a magazine and told people how to fix up their cars. Then he was on television talking about cars and he was a judge for famous cars shows.

The third elaboration further supports the topic sentence that said Phil Hill liked old cars.

For example, Phil Hill was the judge for a car show in California. My dad went to that show and he was looking at the cars on the golf course at Pebble Beach. It was the fortieth time Phil Hill had been the judge there.

I won't ever get to meet Phil Hill, but that is the most famous person I would have liked to meet. I still think he was more important than the NASCAR guys.

Expository Prompt and Writing Activity
(with elaboration)

Read the prompt. Then imagine that the words in italics are the words your teacher is saying to you. Write your essay on a separate sheet of paper. Include at least 15 sentences!

Prompt ➡ Almost every child has been on a class field trip. Think about a trip you were on where you learned new and interesting things. Write an essay to explain what you learned on a class field trip.

Introduction: *Think of a question you could use to begin your essay. Write it first. Then write two more sentences. You can tell when you went on the trip and where your class went.*

Body: *Finish this sentence:* The first thing I learned was . . . *Then write at least two more sentences to explain what you learned about.*

Elaboration: *Hit the "pause button"! You need to tell more. Choose a transition phrase to begin the next paragraph where you will tell more about the first thing you learned.*

Transition Phrases . . .
• When we were . . .
• When the man (woman) said . . .
• We all thought . . .
• When they were almost finished . . .
• In the lesson they said that . . .
• I remember when . . .
• The best part about this was . . .

Body: *Finish this sentence:* We also learned . . . *Then write at least two more sentences to explain something else you learned about.*

Elaboration: *Hit the "pause button"! You need to tell more. Choose another transition phrase to begin the next paragraph where you will tell more about the second thing you learned.*

Body: *Finish this sentence:* Another interesting thing was when we found out . . . *Then write at least two more sentences to explain one more thing you learned about.*

Elaboration: *Hit the "pause button"! You need to tell more. Choose a third transition phrase to begin the next paragraph where you will tell more about the third thing you learned.*

Closing: *Reread your introduction. Now try to write at least two closing sentences so you will be writing in a circle.*

Descriptive Prompt

Prompt ➜ Almost everyone knows of places that are special. Think about a place you have been or have always wanted to visit. Write an essay to describe that place or a part of it.

Introduction (and closing)

Where is the place? What is it called? Where is it? How would you get there?

What does the place look like?

You can describe all of it or only a part. What does it look like? Sound like? Smell like? Feel like? Taste like?

Describe how this place makes you feel.

Describe something you could do in this place.

Descriptive Essay Activity
(no elaboration)

Use a blue crayon, marker, or colored pencil to mark Gil's description of Disney World.

1. Draw a square around the part of Disney World that Gil likes the most.

2. Underline the first sentence in each paragraph of the body of the essay. These are each the topic sentences.

3. Did Gil write in a circle? Draw a star over the words in the introduction that match the words in the closing.

4. Gil also put in his opinion about something, and he mentioned an emotion. Circle the places where you can find an opinion and an emotion word.

"A Special Place" by Gil

The place I would love to go is Disney World. I especially want to go to EPCOT. I don't want to go to the Magic Kingdom because only babies like that place.

The best place in EPCOT is Spaceship Earth. It is located in the enormous ball that you see on all the EPCOT signs. And that ball is huge. You can walk under it and when you look up, it looks like the top of it is as high as airplanes fly.

The outside of Spaceship Earth is beautiful. It is all silver triangles that shine in the bright Florida sun. When I went there, there was a big Mickey Mouse hand and a magic wand on the outside, but I don't think it is there every day. It lights up at night too.

Inside the spaceship everyone rides in little blue cars. It is pitch black in there and the ride goes up, up, and up some more. I think the ride goes clear to the top of the ball, but it is not scary. Then it turns around and you go slowly back down and outside. While you are riding, you hear some man talking about spacemen, telephones, radios, TVs, computers, and other stuff. It has people inside too, but you can tell they are really fake.

I think EPCOT is the best part of Disney World and Spaceship Earth is the most exciting part of EPCOT.

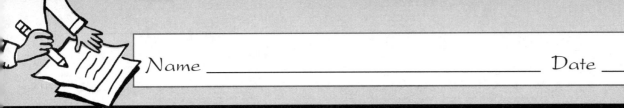

Descriptive Prompt and Writing Activity

(no elaboration)

Read the prompt. Then imagine that the words in italics are the words your teacher is saying to you. Write your essay with at least 15 sentences!

Prompt ➜ Almost everyone has an object that is special. Think about something you have that you really love. Write an essay to describe an object that is special to you.

Introduction: *Think of a question you could use to begin your essay. Write it first. Then write two more sentences. Be sure you write the name of the object that is special. You might also tell where you got it or where you keep it in your house.*

Body: *Finish this sentence by writing one describing word such as "beautiful," "old," "fancy," "beat up," or "uneven."* My _____ is very _____ . *Then write at least two more sentences to describe why that is a good word to describe your object. What makes it beautiful? How is it all beat up? Use all five of your senses to tell about its size, shape, and appearance. You can also tell what it is made of.*

Body: *Finish this sentence:* When I hold my . . . *Then write at least two more sentences to explain more about what you can do with this object. Is it something that you save on a shelf, or play with every day, or use on special occasions, or show to special people? Does your object do anything? Does it make noise or move in any way?*

Body: *Finish this sentence:* I feel very _____ when . . . *Then write at least two more sentences to describe your emotions about this object. Does it make you happy? Excited? How do you feel about it when you see it, wear it, or play with it?*

Closing: *Reread your introduction. Write a closing that includes at least one thing that you used in your introduction. You can use a question, a quotation, a sound word, or just a simple sentence or two to end your essay.*

Descriptive Essay Activity
(with elaboration)

"A Special Place" by Gil

The place I would love to go is Disney World. I especially want to go to EPCOT. I don't want to go to the Magic Kingdom because only babies like that place.

The best place in EPCOT is Spaceship Earth. It is located in the enormous ball that you see on all the EPCOT signs. And that ball is huge. You can walk under it and when you look up, it looks like the top of it is as high as airplanes fly.

The first elaboration is about the music of EPCOT.

When you are walking around EPCOT, there is always great music playing, but you can't see where it is coming from. The music under Spaceship Earth is really great because it is the first thing you see and hear when you enter the park. It sort of gets you in the mood for the whole day.

The outside of Spaceship Earth is beautiful. It is all silver triangles that shine in the bright Florida sun. When I went there, there was a big Mickey Mouse hand and a magic wand on the outside, but I don't think it is there every day. It lights up at night too.

The second elaboration is about the colors of Spaceship Earth, but it also tells you how the lights and sparks make the writer feel.

All of Spaceship Earth is prettier at night. It turns all blue and purple and red. When I looked up, I could even see sparks flying out of the magic wand in the Mickey hand. I could hardly breathe, it was so exciting.

Inside the spaceship everyone rides in little blue cars. It is pitch black in there and the ride goes up, up, and up some more. I think the ride goes clear to the top of the ball, but it is not scary. Then it turns around and you go slowly back down and outside. While you are riding, you hear some man talking about spacemen, telephones, radios, TVs, computers, and other stuff. It has people inside too, but you can tell they are really fake.

The third elaboration is a vignette, or a mini-story, about a time the writer went to EPCOT.

The last time I went on this ride, I was with my dorky little sister. She was screaming and crying the whole time. Embarrassing? You bet! Then when we got off, she wanted to go again!

I think EPCOT is the best part of Disney World and Spaceship Earth is the most exciting part of EPCOT.

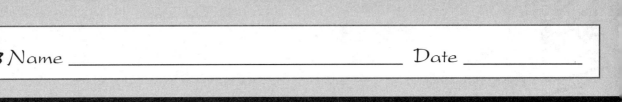
Descriptive Prompt and Writing Activity
(with elaboration)

Read the prompt. Then imagine that the words in italics are the words your teacher is saying to you. Write your essay on a separate sheet of paper. Include three paragraphs in the body and three elaboration paragraphs.

Prompt ➡ Many families have special food for special occasions. Think about the best food you ever ate. Write an essay to describe the best meal you ever had.

Introduction: *Think of something you might say if you just ate something great. Would you say, "Yummy!"? "That's delicious!"? Write what you might say and then add two more sentences to complete your introduction. For example:* _____ ! That is what I said when . . .

Body: *Write a sentence to tell where you were and who you were with when you ate this food. Was it a special occasion? Were you on vacation? Were you at the home of a family? Include at least three sentences. Try beginning this way:* I was at _____ with _____.

Elaboration: *Hit the pause button. Before you tell all about the food, give a little more description about the place where you are eating. Did you order the food, or did you just choose it from a buffet? Are you going to have a whole meal or just desserts?*

Body: *Now tell about the best part you ate. Finish this first sentence with one great describing word:* The _____ was _____! *Then tell more: How big was it? Was it decorated in any way? Was it a special color? How many servings did you have?*

Elaboration: *Hit the pause button again! Now you need to describe how you felt when you ate this food. Were you happy? Did it remind you of something? Did it make you want to dance? This may be difficult, but remember that it doesn't have to be entirely true. For example:* When I tasted the _____ I felt _____.

Body: *Why was this the best food you have ever had? What can you compare it to? What was really special about it? The spices? The sweetness? An unusual ingredient? Include three sentences. Try beginning this way:* I loved the _____ because of the _____.

Elaboration: *Hit the pause button one last time. What was the single most memorable thing about the meal? For example:* I will always remember that . . .

Closing: *Now end your essay by writing in a circle. The closing should have at least one word that was also in the introduction. A good closing will be more than one sentence.*

Transition Phrases

Use a transition phrase to get from one paragraph to the next. These words can be the first word in a sentence or the first word in a paragraph.

Best transition phrases for personal narratives

Event #1 Use one of these just after the introduction to start telling your story:

- I was just
- One day (afternoon, or night)
- Last summer (night, week, year, Thanksgiving)
- When I was only ____ (six, three, a baby)
- While I was
- When we were

Event #2 These words help you tell about the main event in the story:

- Then
- When
- Next
- Suddenly
- Whenever
- Soon
- While I was
- I decided to
- We all thought
- They said

Event #3 At the end of the story, choose one of these words or phrases to start your paragraph:

- Finally
- At last
- When we were finished
- At the end of the day (night, party, class, meeting)
- We decided to
- The best part

Best transition phrases for the expository and descriptive elaborations

Size:
- The smallest
- The largest
- The tallest
- The heaviest
- The lightest
- The biggest
- The tiniest

Importance:
- The best
- The least
- The most important
- The worst
- The first
- The second
- The last

Time:
- Two weeks later
- Yesterday
- Today
- The next day
- Six months later
- I remember when
- Then

Linking events:
- The opposite of ____
- In the first place
- Still
- Although
- For example
- For instance
- Another example
- One time

More transition words:
- The other
- First
- Second
- Third
- Next
- Afterward
- Another reason
- My favorite
- Whenever

Ending transition words:
- Finally
- Last of all
- Now you know
- At last

CHAPTER 4

Using Words Wisely

tate writing assessments are typically scored on either four or six criteria. Scorers are either looking at the four most basic elements (focus, organization, support, and conventions of print) or at six key writing traits (ideas, organization, voice, word choice, sentence fluency, and conventions).

It is important that students write on the assigned topic and it is important they show they are organized and can use correct print conventions effectively. But the most important element for raising a score is having adequate "support" or "content." It is here that the students add details of the events of the story, elaborations in support of a theme, or great description.

There are three basic "tricks of the trade" that are used by professional authors to jazz up their writing and make readers keep turning the pages. These tricks are: the use of figurative language, writing with strong verbs, adverbs, and adjectives, and including a lot of details.

It will do no good at all to simply list these tricks on a bulletin board and tell students to use them. These must be explicitly taught in focused lessons.

LESSON 10

Develop a Vivid Vocabulary

In this lesson students will create their own version of "Big" from *Making Friends With Frankenstein* by Colin McNaughton (Candlewick Press, 1994).

Lesson Preparation: Make copies of the "I'm Talking __ !" template (page 74). Present this lesson using an overhead projector, chart paper, or interactive whiteboard—as long as there is a way to write words in the blank spaces. For the whole-group activity, I usually make this poem—with the blanks—on chart paper so I can write on it and later display it in the classroom as an example for the children to follow.

Make sure you have some dictionaries, a few thesauruses, and/or access to computers with word processing capability or an Internet connection.

This activity works well across two days.

Day 1

STEP 1

Begin by having students read "I'm Talking Scary!" It is great fun to have the whole class read in a scary voice while you point to each word. Some students may enjoy this funny poem without even realizing that nearly every word in it is a synonym for scary.

"I'm Talking Scary!"

I'm talking freaky!

I'm talking frightening!

I'm talking evil, creepy, eerie!

I'm talking fearful, alarming, spooky, startling!

I'm talking terrifying, violent, vicious, powerful, dreadful!

I'm talking terrorizing, awful, terrible, appalling, strange, dangerous!

I'm talking shocking, harsh, horrifying, haunted, deadly, harmful, ghastly!

I'm talking scary!

STEP 2

Next have students brainstorm a list of boring adjectives that they often use in their writing. They will probably list words such as *nice, pretty, fun, loud, little, bad,* and *scary*. Show students the reproducible (page 74) that you made on chart paper and point out the number of blanks for each sentence. Choose a boring adjective and put it at the top of the chart. Then ask students if they can help you think of other words that mean the same, or nearly the same, as your boring word. (See the example in Step 1.)

 Help for struggling and inexperienced writers

Students can't always find 27 synonyms for their boring word. When that happens, you can double-check and give them some assistance, but you can also shorten the poem. Just eliminating the last line will delete seven blanks and make the task easier for students.

■ Your class will probably not be able to come up with all 27 words, so in a few minutes you can pass out a thesaurus and a dictionary to every two or three students.

STEP 3

Have students look up the boring word at the top of the chart. Then have them continue to look up other words that the class has already thought of. As they do so, they should find more and more synonyms for the boring word. Complete the chart as a whole-group activity.

■ If you have computer access, especially hooked to a television screen or interactive whiteboard, demonstrate how to open a word processing document, go to "tools" at the top of the page and click on "thesaurus." After you type in the boring word, you will see lots of synonyms for it, and they can help you choose which ones to use.

■ If you have Internet access, go to a school-approved dictionary or thesaurus site to find even more synonyms for the word.

Day 2

STEP 1

Review "I'm Talking Scary!" from Day 1 and reread the chart you created as a whole group.

STEP 2

Next, divide the class into pairs and ask each student pair to select one of the words from the brainstormed list of boring words or to think of their own boring word. Give each pair a thesaurus, a dictionary (if possible, access to a computer), and two copies of the poem handout (page 74). Both students will work together on the same word, but should each record the poem to keep in their own writing folder.

Help for struggling and inexperienced writers

Encourage students to illustrate their poems and display them in the classroom. It is really helpful for struggling writers to see these synonyms displayed. They will often refer to these charts because they made them themselves.

STEP 3

Have students write a poem of their own that's similar to "I'm Talking Scary!" only have them write it using synonyms for their own boring word. You may have to review the lesson on how to look up words in a thesaurus, and you may have to show them how to type in their word in a word processing document and then click on "thesaurus" to find alternatives.

Allow enough time for students to do a good job on this project, which means that they may require more than one writing class to complete their poems. Encourage students to read their completed poems out loud to the class.

LESSON 11

Degrees of Adjectives

Have your students ever used their adjectives inappropriately? This is not to say that they are totally wrong, but just a little disconcerting in some way. ("I saw a beautiful hamburger.") This lesson focuses on degrees of adjectives because, while synonyms mean *almost* the same thing, they often have subtle differences. *Scared* is not quite the same as *horrified* or *terrified*. *Ugly* is not quite the same thing as *hideous* or *grotesque*. This activity works well using a word from the activity in Lesson 10.

STEP 1

Display the figure from page 75 on the board, a transparency, or chart paper. On the top line, write one of the words from the previous activity or choose one of your own. (We have included an example for *pretty* on page 64.)

STEP 2

For example, if you use the word *pretty*, ask students to brainstorm a list of synonyms. They may think of words such as *beautiful, stunning, breathtaking, gorgeous, lovely, cute,* and *attractive.*

STEP 3

Now ask students to choose a word from the list that they think is the least degree of pretty. They may choose *attractive* or *cute*. Write whatever word they choose at the lowest level of *pretty* on the bottom left-hand corner.

STEP 4

Then ask which of those words means the *most* pretty of them all. That word (probably *stunning, breathtaking,* or *gorgeous*) goes on the top right-hand line.

STEP 5

The next task is for the group to decide where all of the other adjectives belong. As the students make these suggestions collectively, you should fill in the blanks and mediate the discussion.

A sample chart may look something like this:

PRETTY

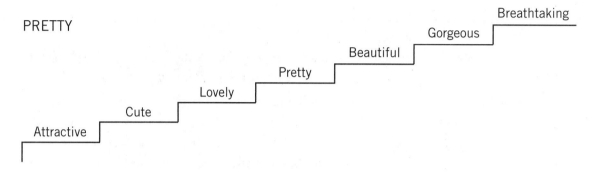

STEP 6

Create some nonsense sentences to help students see that while synonyms mean almost the same thing, using the wrong one can give readers a false impression of what you are trying to describe or, worse yet, make you look like a less capable writer. (Examples: It was a breathtaking hamburger. The lake was cute.)

STEP 7

Have students repeat this activity in small groups using another word of their choice. Make sure they have access to a thesaurus, dictionary, or a computer with word processing capabilities. Each student should record the adjectives on a copy of page 75 to keep in their writing folder.

You may or may not want to extend this project and assign students to repeat this activity individually. On the other hand, if your students are already pretty strong writers, you may want to skip the small-group activity and jump straight to the independent work.

LESSON 12

Figurative Language — SHAMPOPI

Make sure your students understand the difference between literal and figurative language. The words in literal language do not deviate from their actual meanings. If the writer writes, "He is stirring the pot," he means just that: there is a person using an implement to move around the contents of a pot. When reading figurative language, we do not take the words at face value. "He is stirring the pot" would mean that the person was "stirring up" trouble or causing conflict of some kind. Figurative language is what makes writing come alive and keeps the reader turning

the pages. Most students are capable of using at least a few of the eight main types of figurative language.

One way to help students remember the types of figurative language is to give them the acronym SHAMPOPI (pronounced "sham-POP-ee").

Lesson Preparation: Make copies of pages 76 and 77 for each student. Write SHAMPOPI vertically on the left-hand side of a piece of chart paper. Plan to display the completed chart in your classroom.

STEP 1

Explain to students that one of the ways professional authors make their writing come alive and remain interesting, even when the story is more than 100 pages long, is by using figurative language.

STEP 2

Give your students the following examples to help them to see that a literal phrase is factual—the words accurately describe details—while in figurative language, the meaning of the words differs from their literal meaning.

LITERAL	The man was 100 years old.	The room was very warm.	Your brother likes to swim.	My voice is raspy today.
FIGURATIVE	That guy was as old as the hills.	It was so hot in there I was boiling!	Your brother is a fish.	I have a frog in my throat.

STEP 3

Ask students for examples of places where they would probably find only literal writing (science book, social studies book, *National Geographic*, math books, science fair exhibit, newspapers) and examples of places where they are likely to find figurative language (jokes, some magazines, literature, plays, poetry).

STEP 4

Present the Figurative Language reference sheet (page 76) and have students practice saying "SHAMPOPI." Tell them they can use this funny word to help them remember the main kinds of figurative language. Then go down the chart, explain what each letter stands for, and see if you and the whole class can think of examples of each kind of language.

■ It may take several days to do this! Hint: If you know that your students are about to read a passage that has great metaphors in it, do that part of the lesson right before they tackle that particular part of the story.

STEP 5

Look back at the four examples of figurative language in the chart. Ask students if they can determine which kind of figurative language each one represents. (The guy was as old as the hills—simile; It was so hot in there I was boiling—hyperbole; Your brother is a fish—metaphor; I have a frog in my throat—idiom)

STEP 6

Display the chart in a prominent place in your classroom. Continue to add to it, especially if you hear a child using figurative language in a casual conversation. Children need to recognize that figurative language is oral, as well as written.

Have students complete page 77 and keep it in their writing folders. Students can also create eight pages, each with the name of one kind of figurative writing written at the top. Throughout the school year, have students collect examples of different types of figurative language and add them to the appropriate page.

LESSON 13

Similes

The simile is the most commonly used type of figurative language. Even beginning writers have little trouble learning to understand, recognize, and use similes in their independent writing.

> **DEFINITION:** A simile is a comparison using *like* or *as*.
> **EXAMPLES:** The corn tasted as sweet as honey. The dog was as black as night.

Lesson Preparation: Purchase a bag of colorful cap erasers or other small kid-friendly items, such as sticky notes, pencils, gel pens, polished rocks, magnets, or spider rings. The trick is to hold up something that will spark the interest of your students and make them want to participate in the activity. Before class, write these simile starters on the board or on a sheet of chart paper:

- This cap eraser is like a _____ .

- A cap eraser is as _____ as a _____ .

Be sure to leave space to record students' answers. Reveal only one phrase at a time.

STEP 1

Show students a bag of cap erasers and tell them you will be happy to share. Any child who finishes the following sentence will be given an eraser to keep.

This cap eraser is like a _____ .

STEP 2

As students offer suggestions, the teacher records their ideas on a chart and gives an eraser to each child who provides a suitable word or phrase. Examples:

My cap eraser is like a red rocket.

My cap eraser is like a cherry Popsicle.

My cap eraser is like a closed mushroom.

STEP 3

After everyone in the class has received one eraser, tell students that they can earn a second one if they help you complete the next sentence:

A cap eraser is as _____ as a _____ .

STEP 4

Once again, give an eraser to each child who contributes to the chart.

EXAMPLES:

A cap eraser is as pointy as a sharp pencil.

A cap eraser is as soft as a doughnut.

A cap eraser is as red as an apple.

STEP 5

When both charts are complete, ask students to look at each one and identify what words all of the examples have in common. They will immediately notice that certain words are repeated over and over again. (The sentences on the first chart always contain the word *like*; those on the second chart always contain *as* _____ *as a* _____ .)

 Help for struggling and inexperienced writers

Try to make sure that every child earns a reward. You can do this by first calling on students who usually struggle, since it becomes more difficult to come up with comparisons after all the obvious ones are taken. Depending on the reward you are using, you can also guide students by asking how the object tastes, feels, looks, sounds, or smells.

Now you can tell students that they have just learned how to write similes. Give them this definition: "A simile is a comparison using *like* or *as*." Now that they have done the activity, they will really understand what a simile is.

To reinforce how to use this type of figurative language, have students complete page 78 and keep it in their writing folder. Be sure to display your charts and encourage students to collect samples of similes as they read. You can also help by pointing out similes when you read aloud to the class.

LESSON 14

Strong Verbs

Share some simple definitions and examples of key parts of speech:

DEFINITION: A noun is a word that names a person, place, or thing.
EXAMPLES: *teacher, school, desk, dog*

DEFINITION: A verb is a word that shows action or being.
EXAMPLES: *eat, run* (action); *was, is* (being)

DEFINITION: An adjective is a word that modifies (or describes) a noun.
EXAMPLES: *kind, new, strong, hungry*

DEFINITION: An adverb is a word that modifies (or describes) a verb.
EXAMPLES: *quickly, slowly*

It's also important to remind students that we can combine nouns and adjectives: *It is a new school. The strong desk did not break. The hungry dog barked.* Point out how each adjective describes the noun. We can also combine verbs and adverbs: *He will eat very quickly. She ran slowly.* Both *quickly* and *slowly* describe, or tell how, the children moved. Use the reproducibles on pages 79 and 80 to help with this lesson.

STEP 1

Begin with verbs. Remind students that authors take great care when choosing which verb to use in their sentences. Certain words will evoke fear, laughter, surprise, or any of a host of emotions in the reader.

STEP 2

Share these examples of great verb choices found in some popular children's books:

■ As Shredderman was climbing up the side of a building, the author shows the character's fear by writing, "I <u>glued</u> my eyes to the air conditioner." (*Shredderman: Secret Identity* by Wendelin Van Draanen, page 88, Scholastic Inc., 2006)

■ J.K. Rowling describes a very plump Dudley hurrying toward Harry Potter this way: "Dudley came <u>waddling</u> toward them as fast as he could." To show the force of a storm and a frightened Harry, she wrote, "The <u>whole shack shivered</u> and Harry <u>sat bolt upright</u>, staring at the door. Someone was outside, knocking to come in." (*Harry Potter and the Sorcerer's Stone* by J.K. Rowling, page 28 and page 45, Scholastic Inc., 1999)

■ When Dana Matherson gets his feet caught in mousetraps, Carl Hiaasen describes the scene this way: "The boy kept his head down and seemed to be in a hurry, though he wasn't running in a normal way; <u>it was more of a wobbly lurch</u>. Each step made a sharp clacking sound that echoed on the pavement." (*Hoot* by Carl Hiaasen, page 193, Alfred A. Knopf, 2002)

STEP 3

Challenge students to identify examples of great verb choices by their favorite authors.

There is no better way to make them aware of the power of words than to help them recognize that those words can convey pain, fear, hope, love, humor, or hatred. Be sure to identify these great verbs when your students are studying a novel or short story. Have students keep lists of great verbs in their writing folders and encourage them to consult these during writing class. Students can begin their lists by recording alternatives to *walk* and *said* (see page 79).

𝓔**xploring ways to move:** Have half of your students line up on one side of the classroom. Then tell them that you would like for them to walk across the room to the other side. Write the word *walk* on the board or chart paper. Then ask them to hop back across the classroom. Write the word *hop* on the board or chart paper. Ask the students who remained in their seats to think of another verb to describe a way of crossing the room. For each creative movement these students suggest, have the standing students demonstrate that type of movement as you add the word to the list. Continue until you have about ten verbs. Then have the students switch places so that all of the students get a chance to do the moving. A sample list might

include words like *run, twirl, crawl, saunter, amble, skip, jump, slither, stroll,* and *leap.*

Have students work together in small groups to continue to list ways that a person or animal might move. Add the words from the various groups until you have a long master list of verbs.

Challenge students to help you sort these words into groups that might show different kinds of emotion. Make sure students realize that the words can be used in more than one way, for example, the word *dash* might be used to indicate speed, but it might also be used to describe the movement of someone who is afraid or feels happy. Here are some possible ways to sort words by emotion:

Fear	Humor	Happiness
slither	wiggle	stroll
slink	waddle	skip
slide	clambered	twirl
sneak	jostled	soar

Exploring ways to speak: On the board write, *"Tomorrow is Friday," said Michael.* Then ask the class to think of alternative words that could replace the word *said*. Try to identify the circumstances in which Michael would have used each one. If the students want to say, *"Tomorrow is Friday," screamed Michael*, they could indicate that Michael fears the coming day. Under what other circumstances would Michael be screaming that it is Friday? Excitement? Dread? Worry? What kinds of words could replace *said* to show excitement, suspense, anger, delight?

Once again, help students to not only make a list of words to replace *said*, but also to recognize when to use those words to help create a mood for their character. Make sure that, just as in the verb activity, their replacements for *said* indicate very different emotions. For example, *"Tomorrow is Friday," whispered Michael,* could mean that he was excited, scared, happy, or worried.

Exploring adverbs: Spend some time reviewing the difference between an adjective and adverb. An adjective should not modify a verb. "He is going to eat slow" and "She is going to run quick," are both incorrect because *slow* and *quick* are adjectives. "The turtle is slow" is correct, because *slow* is describing a noun: the turtle. One could write, "The rabbit is quick," because *quick* describes the rabbit. But if we want to tell how the animals are moving, then we are describing action, so we need an adverb. We can say, "The turtle is slow. The turtle moved slowly." "The rabbit is quick. The rabbit ran quickly." There are exceptions, of course, but generally we need the *-ly* adverb to describe action.

Hand out copies of page 80. Students should fill in the necessary adverbs and keep the page in their writing folders for reference.

LESSON 15

Describing Details

Simply telling students to include lots of details in their writing will seldom get you the results you desire. One way to improve students' attention to detail is to teach them these three tricks about description.

1. When describing a person, start at the head and work your way down to the feet.

2. When describing an animal, begin at the nose and end at the tail.

3. When describing a scene or a room, begin at one side or in one corner and go all around the space, as if you are slowly moving your head and telling what you see.

This activity works well across three days.

Lesson Preparation: Collect some objects for students to describe: stuffed animals (borrow some from the kindergarten class if you don't have any), small action figures or dolls, storybook or cartoon characters—even a photograph or advertisement will do. (As an alternative you could provide popular picture books and have students describe the characters. "Describe Miss Viola Swamp or the Cat in the Hat!") Place all of the objects in a large bag so that students cannot see them. You will need enough items so that you can do one whole-group lesson and be able to provide one item for each small group.

Day 1

STEP 1

Remove one object from the bag and place it in front of the class. (Begin with the largest object so that all students can see it well.)

STEP 2

Then ask students to describe this figure either from the head to the tail or the head to the feet.

STEP 3

As they offer suggestions, record what they say on a chart, chalkboard, or interactive whiteboard. Encourage students to include as many elements of good description as they can. For example, you may ask students to make sure the completed paragraph contains at least one simile and one or two examples of strong verbs or adjectives.

■ Be sure to circle these or write them in a different color so that students are fully aware of the value they add to the paragraph.

■ Let students have fun with this activity.

Day 2

STEP 1

Put students into groups. Allow one person from each group to choose an item from the bag.

STEP 2

Have each group of students work together to write a descriptive paragraph about the item.

STEP 3

Once again, suggest that they use some figurative language (hyperbole is easy, so are similes) and to include strong verbs and adjectives. Encourage students to refer to the word lists they have created throughout the lessons in this chapter.

STEP 4

Allow each group to read its paragraph aloud to the class.

STEP 5

As a homework assignment, ask students to bring in an item that they would like to describe.

Day 3

STEP 1

During the next writing session, give students time to write a full description of the item. (Or if you are brave, allow them to exchange items during the writing time—but they have to return the items!)

STEP 2

Encourage students to include strong verbs, adverbs, and adjectives and to describe from the head to the feet or the head to the tail.

Display the completed descriptive paragraphs with the items—or for even more fun, display all of the items, select a descriptive paragraph, and see if the students can determine which item you are describing, just by listening to the description.

Review

Review the concepts covered in this chapter, with a particular focus on figurative language.

Use page 81 as a whole-group review, a small-group activity, independent work, or an assessment.

Answers: *Strong verbs:* staggered, shrieked, splattering, clonking, spilled, striping, pooling; The paint "ran in rivers" is a metaphor that means the paint ran in long stripes across his clothes. *Adjectives for Grandma:* ready-made dress, covered with flowers, fine net, big cameo, large, unfamiliar shoes, white big, perky bows, big brim, blue ribbon. Since the children in the story see Grandma all dressed up, which was a very rare occasion, "striking us dumb" actually means that they were so stunned that they could not speak. "Dumb" is an antiquated word meaning that someone could not speak, not that they are unintelligent. This is an idiom.

Use page 82 as extra practice with figurative language—and as another reference sheet for students' writing folders. You can make this page more difficult by folding back the suggested word list at the bottom of the page, before you make copies. You can make it slightly easier by marking out the words *personification* and *paradox*, which are not used for this activity.

Answers: 1. alliteration 2. alliteration 3. idiom 4. idiom 5. onomatopoeia 6. metaphor 7. hyperbole 8. simile 9. hyperbole 10. alliteration.

I'm Talking ____!

Use this poetry frame to replace a boring adjective with some that are more interesting or precise.

Write a boring word here: _____

I'm talking _____ !

I'm talking _____ !

I'm talking _____ , _____ !

I'm talking _____ , _____ !

I'm talking _____ , _____ , _____ !

I'm talking _____ , _____ , _____ !

I'm talking _____ !

Name _____ Date _____

Degrees of Adjectives

Write an adjective here: _____

Now write at least six synonyms for that adjective.

_____ _____

_____ _____

_____

Rewrite the starting adjective on the line below. Then arrange the synonyms in order from least intense to the most intense.

Least

Most

Figurative Language

Here are eight kinds of figurative language and examples of each one.

INITIAL	FIGURATIVE LANGUAGE	DEFINITION	EXAMPLES
S	**Simile**	a comparison that uses *like* or *as*	He looked like a drowned rat. She looked like a princess. It was as cold as ice. The sidewalk was as hot as a firecracker.
H	**Hyperbole**	deliberate and obvious exaggeration	I am freezing to death in here! That cake is to die for!
A	**Alliteration**	repeated use of an initial letter	Sammie was lost in the deep, dark dungeon. Peter Piper picked a peck of pickled peppers.
M	**Metaphor**	a comparison that does not use *like* or *as*	That Joe is a snake! You hit a home run with your great idea.
P	**Personification**	when we give human characteristics to an object or idea	The wind shrieked. The table groaned under the weight of the feast.
O	**Onomatopoeia**	a word that sounds like the sound it is describing	*Hiss* and *buzz* are examples of onomatopoeia; crash is just a sound word. The bee buzzed around the flower.
P	**Paradox**	putting two contradictory qualities together	His spelling was poor, but his writing was rich. The light was dim, but her smile was bright.
I	**Idiom**	a colorful and commonly used expression that means something different from what it appears to mean	It is raining cats and dogs. His jokes had me in stitches. Learning to play checkers is as easy as rolling off a log.

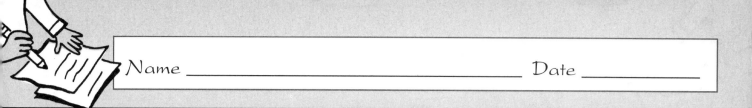

Remembering Types of Figurative Language

After each definition of a type of figurative language, write your own example. It can be something you make up, something you found in a book, or a familiar phrase. Can you think of more than one example of each type? Can you make up your own?

INITIAL	FIGURATIVE LANGUAGE	DEFINITION	EXAMPLES
S	**Simile**	a comparison that uses *like* or *as*	
H	**Hyperbole**	deliberate and obvious exaggeration	
A	**Alliteration**	repeated use of an initial letter	
M	**Metaphor**	a comparison that does not use *like* or *as*	
P	**Personification**	when we give human characteristics to an object or idea	
O	**Onomatopoeia**	a word that sounds like the sound it is describing	
P	**Paradox**	putting two contradictory qualities together	
I	**Idiom**	a colorful and commonly used expression that means something different from what it appears to mean	

Similes

Remember, a simile is a comparison using *like* or *as*. Make up five examples of each and write them below.

My _____ is like a _____ .

My _____ is like a _____ .

My _____ is like a _____ .

My _____ is like a _____ .

My _____ is like a _____ .

My _____ is as _____

as a _____ .

My _____ is as _____

as a _____ .

My _____ is as _____

as a _____ .

My _____ is as _____

as a _____ .

My _____ is as _____

as a _____ .

Using Words Wisely:
Verbs

How do you move when . . . ? (WALK)

you are scared

_____

_____

you are in a hurry

_____

_____

you are sneaking

_____

_____

something is funny

_____

_____

you are not in a hurry

_____

_____

you are disappointed

_____

_____

you feel happy

_____

_____

you feel dread

_____

_____

you get an award

_____

_____

How do you speak when . . . ? (SAID)

you are scared

_____

_____

you are in a hurry

_____

_____

you are being sneaky

_____

_____

you are being funny

_____

_____

you are being quiet

_____

_____

you are lying

_____

_____

you feel happy

_____

_____

you are excited

_____

_____

you are angry

_____

_____

Using Words Wisely:

Adverbs

An adverb describes a verb. Think of an action word like *race*. Now think about how a person might race. We might say, "Ann raced quickly" or that "Arthur raced clumsily." In these sentences, *quickly* and *clumsily* are both adverbs because they describe the verb *race*.

Circle the action word (verb). Then write an adverb in each of the blanks. Be creative and make the sentences interesting or amusing. Try not to use the same adverb more than once.

1. Jenna ran _____ across the field to catch the ball.

2. Zach jumped _____ when he heard the thunder.

3. Ivania sang _____ in the church.

4. Nicholas hopped _____ into the car.

5. John looked _____ at the brownies.

6. Ryan worked _____ on the puzzle.

7. Nancy _____ combed her hair.

8. Margie _____ cooked breakfast.

9. Timesha _____ pushed the door.

10. Juan _____ watched the scoreboard.

11. Tom _____ cleaned the pool.

12. Sue _____ paid her bills.

13. Olita read her book _____ .

14. Martha pulled the weeds _____ .

15. Brian walked _____ into the movie theater.

THINK: What do most of these adverbs have in common? _____

Name _____ Date _____

Using Words Wisely:
Details, Strong Verbs and Adjectives, and Figurative Language

Using strong verbs

From *Meet Kit* by Valerie Tripp (page 75, American Girl Publishing Inc., 2000)

"Kit was so angry and shoved so hard that Roger staggered backward, lost his balance, and fell against a ladder that had a bucket of white paint on it. Everyone shrieked in horror and delight as the can fell over, splattering white paint on the backdrop and clonking Roger on the head. White paint spilled over Roger's hair and face and shoulders and back and arms. It ran in rivers down Roger, striping his legs and his socks and pooling into white puddles around his shoes."

The author uses strong verbs in this paragraph. Circle at least four strong verbs.

Write two other verbs that Mrs. Tripp could have used in place of those circled.

_____ , _____

What kind of figurative language is "*[the paint] ran in rivers*"? What does this expression mean?

_____

Describing a person with strong adjectives

From *A Long Way From Chicago* by Richard Peck (page 66, Scholastic Inc., 1998)

"Then Grandma sailed like a galleon into the front room, striking us dumb. For her, dressing up usually meant taking off her apron. But this morning she wore a ready-made dress covered with flowers. The collar was fine net, fixed with a big cameo brooch that rode high. On her feet were large, unfamiliar shoes — white with the hint of a heel, and laces tied in big, perky bows. On her head was a hat with a big brim. The hatband on it happened to be a blue ribbon."

Circle three strong adjectives that describe Grandma.

Write two other adjectives that you think could describe Grandma instead of those circled.

_____ , _____

What kind of figurative language is "striking us dumb"? What does this expression mean?

_____

Using Words Wisely:
Figurative Language

Read the following from "The Poisonous Duck" by Patrick Jennings (from *Storyworks* magazine, January 2008). Identify the figurative language that is underlined. Choose from the answer options in the box.

1. Deadly ducks are heading our way! _____

2. This is exactly the kind of sentence that too often flies out of the mouth of my extremely bizarre big brother, Thaddeus. _____

3. And this is how his stories tend to get: bigger and bigger, till you can't possibly swallow them. _____

4. Wild horses won't keep him from telling me. _____

5. Cluck? Chirp? Caw? Cock-a-doodle-do? _____

6. . . . . my brother's a flake. _____

7. It might mean the extinction of the human race! _____

8. I'm as dumb as a duck. _____

9. The poisonous ducks are here! The end is nigh! _____

10. He's got a big gloaty grin on his face. _____

| hyperbole | alliteration | simile | metaphor |
| personification | idiom | onomatopoeia | paradox |

Self-Editing

Have you ever noticed how easy it is to find the errors others have made in their writing, yet it is difficult to find your own mistakes? This is one reason that many teachers have eliminated "peer editing" in the classroom. Students need to be able to spot their own errors and to improve and revise their writing without the input of others. This chapter will teach your students to edit their work independently.

Practically every teacher in the country agonizes over the mechanical errors made daily by the writers in his or her class. Mechanical errors are those that involve punctuation, capitalization, and spelling. The suggestions given here are intended to help students improve in these areas. They are not, by any means, a surefire panacea, but they should make your job a little easier.

LESSON 16

R.E.A.D.

In this lesson, students will edit their own work. Use the reproducible on page 88 to help with this lesson. If you are lucky enough to have classroom aides or mentors, check out the guidelines on page 89.

> R.E.A.D.
> **R**eread
> **E**rase
> **A**dd
> **D**id?

STEP 1

Ask students to choose a piece of writing from their writing folders, or use a story or an essay that they have recently completed.

STEP 2

Tell students that they are now going to edit their work. After the groans have subsided and you have assured them that editing does not necessarily mean a complete rewrite, write the letters R, E, A, and D on the board vertically.

After the letter R, write the word *reread*.

STEP 3

Point out that the first step to editing is to reread the piece. We don't mean just quickly glancing over the page. What we mean is for the child to point to every word and read each one out loud, slowly and deliberately, listening to the words carefully. You should demonstrate this with a sentence or two.

Why R.E.A.D.?

We use the acronym R.E.A.D. because it is easy to remember and it is what most teachers tell their students to do when they have completed any task. "If you have finished your book report, you may read until lunchtime." "If you complete your math test early, please read silently until others are finished."

Discourage students from sliding their finger across a page of writing; when they do this, they end up reading what they thought they wrote, or what they intended to write, instead of what is actually there. Insist that they touch each word individually and deliberately.

■ This method will help students focus on flow and to hear if the writing makes sense. Errors having to do with conventions of print can be overlooked, but nothing will help if the writing is not clear.

■ Tell students that if they find an error, they should fix it immediately. As they begin to read, your classroom will get quite noisy, but only for a few minutes. Then it will get quieter as students begin to take the task seriously and start correcting errors. To make sure they understand what to do, ask if anyone is willing to tell about a mistake they corrected. Here are some typical responses you'll get: "I forgot to put an "s" on *cats.*" "I had 'the the' in my sentence." "I left out the word *went*, so my sentence said, 'I outside.'"

STEP 4

After the letter E, write *erase*. Most of the students will be expecting you to write *edit*, so they are usually happy to see directions to do something they are really good at: erasing! Instruct students to skim their paper to see if they have used any boring words or expressions. ("It was fun." "I had a good time." "It was big." "I felt happy.") Tell them to erase these boring words and insert more interesting or precise ones. Allow them to refer to the word lists (from Chapter 4) they are keeping in their writing folders or to use a thesaurus to find the right word.

■ Ask students to share with the class what changes they have made. Encourage them to erase in more than one place!

STEP 5

Beside the letter A, write *add*. Here is where you introduce the caret (^). Explain to the class that this symbol is used to insert a new phrase or a word.

Rewriting

There is nothing that children hate more about writing class than having to totally rewrite a piece of work, and there is rarely a justification for asking students to do this. Most of the writing that students do is a learning process, so it does not need to be perfect. Indeed, most of the prompts suggested in this book are used as instructional pieces, not with an eye toward producing published, perfect works. When students are learning to edit and improve their writing, simply store these in writing folders or large manila envelopes.

You can avoid the "total rewrite" by having students use pencils instead of pen. A few messy erasures are OK and are to be expected in student work. You can also allow them to type their stories using computers. While most of us older adults learned to write on paper and then type, even young children are perfectly capable of composing at the computer. And they probably already know how to cut and paste, spell-check, and use the dictionary and thesaurus to improve their work.

Demonstrate how to insert the caret and suggest that they use this mark to insert some describing words, a metaphor, or a simile.

■ Ask several students to read their examples out loud. When struggling writers hear what others have done, it serves as a model for them and helps them to understand the task at hand.

STEP 6

Finally, go to the letter D and write *did?* This is the last step of the editing process, and it is here that the child looks at the closing of the piece and asks, "Did I write in a circle?" Have him or her circle one word, phrase, name, or idea in the introduction and the same word in the closing. This will assure that your student has wrapped up the essay neatly.

 Help for struggling and inexperienced writers

Walk around the room when they are doing the R.E.A.D. process. You can help them read out loud and gently point out what does not make sense. You can also draw a little star or use a mini-sticker to indicate places where the child did a good job of self-correcting.

Covering the whole process may be too much for some students to handle in one lesson. Try doing just the R. part on one story, R.E. on the second story, and R.E.A.D. on the third story.

You will need to R.E.A.D. many, many times before your students do this automatically.

DOES THE WORK NEED A TITLE?

To title or not to title? That is the question. A title on a piece of work conveys the feeling that it is "whole and complete," but in most cases the title does not add to or detract from the score being assigned by a state writing assessment scorer. Here are some guidelines for helping students with titling their work.

Have students add the title *after* the work is complete and has been edited. I once had a child sit for 20 minutes during our state writing assessment without doing any writing. Of course, I was not allowed to help him, but I did ask if there was a problem. He said that he just couldn't think of a title yet. Help your students understand that it is not necessary to have a title to begin—and teach them to add the title last.

Use the reproducible activity on page 90 to teach your students some easy ways to write titles.

SHOULD STUDENTS DOUBLE SPACE?

Discourage students from skipping lines when they are writing. Teachers who allow students to skip lines often do so in the hopes that students will use the spaces between lines to revise and edit their work. Students who were taught to skip lines also tend to skip lines on the state writing assessment. In many states, students are given only one sheet of paper on which to respond to their prompt, so students who skip lines have effectively cut their writing space in half, and it is very difficult to earn a high score in such a limited space.

IS CURSIVE WRITING REQUIRED?

As more and more students work on computer keyboards, the great cursive writing debate rages louder than ever. Several state benchmarks clearly state that students must learn cursive writing. If your state requires this, you will be out of compliance if you omit it from your lessons. A few states demand that the state writing assessment be done in cursive. Before you abandon cursive lessons, make sure that your students will not be marked down for manuscript writing.

Even though we all love the wonderful attributes of word processing, there is nothing quite like a hand-written note, a few words written on a card, a thank-you note, or an invitation. Everyone needs to develop a cursive signature to be used on documents throughout his or her life. Cursive writing has a flow and speed to it that is not usually possible to achieve with manuscript writing. And cursive writing just looks more grown-up!

Some students, however, have such poor fine motor skills that cursive writing is slow, laborious, and difficult to read. If students are working on a timed state writing assessment, cursive writing may actually work against them; they will run out of time, and the combination of poor spelling and poor cursive writing can make the essay illegible.

I would hope that we continue to teach cursive writing, but for the writing assessment, encourage the most struggling writers to abandon cursive in favor of a legible, faster, and easier manuscript. At least the scorer will be able to read the piece!

HOW IMPORTANT IS LEGIBLE HANDWRITING?

Remember that state writing assessment scorers read thousands of essays. When the handwriting is too tiny, too faint, too messy, or otherwise difficult to read, the scorer can often miss the ideas the child is trying to express. Clear handwriting is not just attractive, it is necessary to convey your message. While scorers will usually give students the benefit of a doubt, they will not spend an inordinate amount of time trying to decipher what one of your students is trying to say.

Here are three suggestions for improving your students' handwriting:

- Procure a tablet of large sheets of chart paper with a clear base line and dotted midline between writing lines. Use this paper whenever you are giving a writing demonstration, and remind students how letters should look as you are making them. You may not think this is necessary in the upper elementary grades, but I assure you that it is.
- Ask your school to purchase ruled handwriting paper. This paper usually has blue lines for writing and a dotted midline between them. The baseline (the bottom line on which the letters "sit") is often red.
- Use handwriting paper as often as possible and ask teachers in the lower grades to do the same. Many teachers go to regular lined paper (without the dotted line midline) as early as first grade. These students are often the ones who have the most difficulty forming letters correctly.

INVENTED AND TEXTING SPELLING

When the whole-language method of teaching reading and writing was in vogue, teachers often allowed "invented spelling." Invented spelling is great for use in the primary grades; we cannot and should not expect beginning writers to know how to spell words that are often very confusing in our complex language. Invented spelling is still acceptable in the upper elementary grades, especially with unusual or rarely used words. Allow your students the freedom to spell complicated words— such as restaurant or astronaut, or words derived from other languages with tricky spellings, such as *filet* or *fajita*—as they think they should be spelled, without fear of being harshly corrected.

One more note on spelling: do not allow "texting spelling"—ever. Simply state that it is fine to use when texting, but in the classroom *writing* requires correctly spelled words. If students continue to use this abbreviated style of spelling, consistently take off a point or two, "for spelling"!

Editing Checklist

When you finish your writing, follow these steps to make sure you have done your very best.

❏ Skim your work to find names of people or important places. Make sure each of these has a capital letter.

❏ There is a pattern to writing. Each time you make a period, question mark, or exclamation mark at the end of a sentence, the next letter you make should begin with a capital letter. Count your sentences. Now count your end punctuation. The number should be the same.

❏ You should have at least five paragraphs in your essay. Check to see that you indented five times. Check to see if there are any words that you may have spelled incorrectly (especially spelling review words). Look them up or ask someone if you are unsure.

❏ In formal writing you should not use contractions or abbreviations. Write out the words *did not* for *didn't*. Write out the meaning of acronyms like PTA (Parent-Teacher Association). Do not use "texting spelling"—EVER!

❏ It is important to write neatly. Make sure the reader (your friend, your teacher, a professional scorer) can read your work. On a test, you will lose credit if the scorer has to guess what you are trying to say.

❏ Follow the R.E.A.D. method to help you improve your work.

R **Reread** your entire essay very slowly, making sure to point to every word as you read it. Make corrections if you find any errors.

E Skim through your work to find any places that you have used boring words like the adjectives *good, nice,* or *big*. **Erase** these and replace them with more exciting words like *wonderful, fabulous,* or *enormous*.

A **Add** a describing word or two, or even a descriptive phrase. Use a caret (^) to insert the new words. Reread your sentence to make sure it still makes sense.

D Ask yourself, "**Did** I write in a circle?" If you can find words, ideas, phrases, names, or some other language in the introduction that also appears in the closing, you have written in a circle. This makes your writing seem "whole and complete" and shows the reader that you had a plan for writing.

❏ Add a title. Remember, unless you have an idea right away, it is important to title your work when you are finished writing and editing.

Guidelines for Writing Mentors

1. Ask the student to read his or her story out loud.
Follow closely, because if many of the words are misspelled, you may not be able to read it on your own. Do not point out any other mistakes at this first reading. You are just listening to see if the content makes sense. If the child recognizes an error and wants to change it, allow him or her to do so.

2. Point out some things the child has done well. It may be funny or have several good descriptions. Perhaps the writer has remembered to use capital letters in names, included a title, or written neatly. Remember that students often feel that they are not good writers. Your praise will go a long way in encouraging them to work to improve. If you cannot think of something specific to the piece, at least say, "I can tell you worked really hard on this," or "I am very proud that you were able to write so much today."

3. During an editing session, choose one item from each checklist for your focus.

CONTENT: A student's piece should include each of these elements. Help the child add any that are not yet included.

❏ **writing in a circle** – This means that there should be one word in the first paragraph that is reused in the conclusion.

❏ **use of figurative language** – Look for similes, which are common. This is when we compare things using the words *like* or *as.* Examples: It is glistening like gold. It is as hot as a firecracker.

❏ **use of description** – The writer may include a physical description, especially one that draws upon the five senses—how it looked, sounded, smelled, felt, or tasted. Writers can also describe thoughts, moods, emotions, action, or a scene.

❏ **use of interesting words** – We encourage students to erase boring words such as *good, big,* and *bad* and replace them with more interesting words, such as *spectacular, enormous,* and *awful.*

❏ **title** – We teach students to work on this last in order to keep them focused on the content and conventions of print.

CONVENTIONS OF PRINT: Look for these elements in the piece. Choose one of these items for your focus. Unless the child is a solid, confident writer who makes few errors, do not try to fix all of these at once.

❏ **spelling** – There are certain words that the child should be able to spell by now, like *they, went,* and *goes.* Help students correct these errors. Allow invented spelling to stand if the child has tried to use large, complicated words.

❏ **capitalization** – Help the child to go through the story and look to see if every sentence begins with a capital letter. If he cannot tell where the new sentences begin, have him read it out loud again, and point out that each time he takes a breath is usually where a period belongs. Help him include capital letters on names.

❏ **punctuation** – Help the child to recognize that each time there is a new sentence, the preceding one must end with a period or other punctuation.

4. End by giving the child positive feedback.
Choose one of these examples or think of your own. Whatever you say, make sure it is sincere. You can thank him for his hard work; tell him it is better than his last piece; that you look forward to reading his next story; tell him your favorite part, or anything else he has done well.

Choosing a Title

Unless you are struck with an idea immediately, try to title your work when you are finished writing and editing. That way, if you run out of time, you will still have a good essay and you will not have wasted time thinking of what to call your piece.

The title usually reflects the topic or main idea of the story. Read over these examples of book titles and short story titles and then write your own titles in these styles.

Alliteration: *Brown Bear, Brown Bear, What Do You See?* by Eric Carle; "The Terrible Twisted Tooth" by Zach

In alliterative titles several words begin with the same letter. Write your own alliterative

title here: _____

One-word: *Hoot* by Carl Hiaasen; "Gorilla" by A.J.

Simple, one-word titles can be attention-grabbing. Write your own one-word title here:

_____

Mysterious: *Emma Jean Lazarus Fell Out of a Tree* by Lauren Tarshis; "The Day Was Totally Lost" by Jacqueline

A mysterious title gives little or no hint of what the story is about. Write your own

mysterious title here: _____

Descriptive: *Harry Potter and the Sorcerer's Stone* by J.K. Rowling; "My First Ride on a Horse" by Emma

A descriptive title tells you exactly what the story is about. Write your own descriptive

title here: _____

Time or place: *Where the Wild Things Are* by Maurice Sendak; "Up in the Treehouse" by Ethan

Titles that show time or place help the reader imagine the setting. Write your own title

here: _____

Sample Essay: Narrative

Here is Jenna's response to a narrative prompt. As you read through this essay, look for the following elements that would make this response receive a high score if it were on a state assessment.

❏ title ❏ introduction ❏ extensive description ❏ conversation
❏ voice of the writer ❏ originality ❏ figurative language ❏ closing

Prompt ➜ Everyone has found something. Think about a time that you found an interesting object. Write a story about a time when you found something.

Cowboy Genie by Jenna

I am sure you have found something before! I have. Today I am going to tell you about a time I found something really special!

I was just jumping on my trampoline when something caught my eye. It was gold and shiny! I went over to the bushes and picked it up. It was a lamp, like the one that genies come out of.

It was as golden as gold itself! The handle was made of purple jewels, and so was the bottom of the lamp. It looked as if it just came out of a mini car wash, because it was so shiny.

The top was dusty, so I rubbed the lamp to get the dust off when a . . . um, a cowboy appeared. If anything came out of a lamp, I would have thought it would be a genie! The cowboy yelled, "I am your cowboy genie to grant you nothin' but three, yup three, wishes!" He needed to go to my teacher for some grammar lessons!

I said, "Are you really a genie? I mean, if you were a genie, I would have thought that you would be flying and wearing jewelry and stuff."

He said, "I ain't no girl, am I?"

I examined him. He had a cowboy hat on with wild blonde hair, and a long-sleeved shirt with a red vest. He had on ripped up jeans with brown cowboy boots. He wasn't flying, and he wasn't wearing jewelry.

"Do you trick people with their wishes?" I asked.

"Nope. We cowboys are as straight-shooters, whatever that means."

I said, "Fine. I wish for . . . hum . . . I wish for a puppy, a boat, and a twin sister. All of a sudden, they all appeared in my backyard. My twin sister ran up and hugged me! I said to the genie, "Thank you."

"You're right on welcome," he said. "Now if you will excuse me, I am going to go be a rock star genie!"

Then he transformed into a rock star. I wasn't even surprised. I was too focused on how I was going to tell my parents about my new sister, boat, and puppy!

So now you know about my special genie lamp that I found in my backyard. I wonder what kind of genie I will find next. I could find a surfer genie, a rock star genie, a soccer genie, a Barney genie . . .

Sample Essay: Expository

Here is Jenna's response to an expository prompt. As you read through this essay, look for the following elements that would make this response receive a high score if it were on a state assessment.

❏ title ❏ introduction ❏ extensive description ❏ conversation
❏ voice of the writer ❏ originality ❏ figurative language ❏ closing

Prompt ➜ Who is your favorite family member? Think about why this person is special to you. Write an essay to explain why this person is special to you.

My Special, Special Mother by Jenna

Do you have someone in your life that is very important? I bet you have tons! I know I do! I have my dad, my sister, my brother, and a lot more. But the person I am going to tell you about is my mom.

The first reason my mom is important to me is because she loves me and I love her. She shows me this by giving me a home and cooking meals for me. I could go on and on about her.

I remember when I was little, when I didn't get stuff I wanted, I would cry and cry and cry! If she still didn't give me what I wanted, I felt like she didn't love me. But now that I am older, I understand that she will always love me, no matter what.

Another reason my mom is important is because she is very caring! I know this because when I get hurt, she is always there with her first aid kit! Also when I eat too much junk food, my mom makes sure that I eat some protein. She tried to take care of me in every way.

When I am sick, my mom makes sure I get plenty of rest and medicine. She stays home with me and takes care of me. Last month when I had a bad cold, she made a special soup for me and she kept taking my temperature and giving me Tylenol. She is caring because she was worried when I was sick.

The last reason is that she is very helpful. My mom helps me with my homework, helps me stay focused, and so on. Even though my mom is sometimes busy, she is always there to help.

One time when my mom had just started work for the year, she was as busy as a beaver. But the problem was that I had no clue how to do any of my homework. I tried and tried, but couldn't do it. I tried to find something else to do, but couldn't. Finally at the end of the day, she helped me with all of it.

So now you know how important my mom is to me. She is more than loving, caring, and helpful. She is the BEST mom EVER! I LOVE her so much. Of course she is not the only one. I could go on all day telling about people that are important to me. So the next time your mom cooks for you or takes care of you, or helps you with your homework, think about all the stuff she does for you.

Sample Essay: Descriptive

Here is Jenna's response to a descriptive prompt. As you read through this essay, look for the following elements that would make this response receive a high score if it were on a state assessment.

❏ title ❏ introduction ❏ extensive description ❏ conversation
❏ voice of the writer ❏ originality ❏ figurative language ❏ closing

Prompt ➡ Almost everyone has something that is special to them. What is special to you? Write an essay to tell why something is special to you.

Do you have an object that is special to you? I have lots! But today I am going to tell you about only one. It is my locket.

The first reason I like my locket is because it has my whole family in it. (Except for my pets.) It has a picture of my mom, then my dad. Then you flip something over and it has my sister, then my brother.

I remember, before I had my locket, I always wanted one! Before every holiday, I would say, "I want a locket! It's an idea for a present." Then I finally got one for my birthday and I was excited!

Another reason I LOVE my locket is because of how it looks. It is shaped in a heart, with a cursive "j" on it. It is silver and shiny!

When I first got my locket, I would wear it everywhere! I would show it to all of my friends! But then one day I opened it up, and two of the pictures were gone! I retraced my steps over and over again! I finally found them both. I was very, very lucky. After that I didn't wear it that much anymore because I was afraid that I would lose the pictures.

The last reason I think my locket is special is because it shows how much my family loves me. I know this is true because my family bought that locket for me and it didn't look cheap. I was so happy!

When I got my locket, I felt very loved. To know that my parents went out and took time to buy it for me was really kind. I was very thankful for it and very happy to know that my parents love me.

So now you know why I treasure my locket so much. It is only one thing I treasure though I still have tons of things I think are special to me. I could go on and on, but my hand's getting tired!

Narrative

Everyone knows what it's like to lose a tooth. Think about a time when your tooth came out. Write a story about a time you lost a tooth.

Almost every classroom has one or two interesting science projects. But what would happen if one of those projects went out of control? Write a story about a time when a science project went wrong in your class.

Almost everyone has used a computer to look something up, play a game, or do some homework. What could happen if the computer started acting strangely? Write a story about a time your computer did something weird.

What if you could have a magical power? What would you do with it? Write a story about a time you used a magical power in a special way.

Your friend invites you to come over for dinner. Just as you get to the end of the block, you see a flashing light and hear some loud noises. Write a story about what happens next.

You are shopping with your mom and your best friend when you and your friend wander away from your mom. You look around and realize that it is late, and you have been locked in the store. Write a story about what happens next.

Think about a time that you got to play a game or do an activity outdoors. What happened to make that a game to remember? Write a story that tells what happened one time when you played a game outside.

Almost every child has been on a class field trip. Think about which field trip was your favorite. Write a story about a time your class went on a field trip.

Teachers like to do special things for their students. Think about a time a teacher did something special for you. Write a story about a time a teacher did something special for you or your class.

Almost everyone has been to a party. Think about a party that was especially fun for you. Write a story to tell what happened at a party you attended.

Everyone has had their hair cut. Think about a time your hair was cut. Write a story to tell about a time you got your hair cut.

Nearly everyone has worn a Band-Aid at one time or another. Think about a time you had a small cut or a scrape. Write a story about a time you wore a Band-Aid.

Almost every classroom has had a substitute teacher. Think of what could happen if the substitute were a famous person. Write a story about a time you had a famous person as your substitute teacher.

What if you found a secret message? What did it mean to you? Write a story about a time you found a secret message.

Every child likes to do certain activities after school. Think about a day when you did something fun after school. Write a story about a time you did something fun after school.

Kids enjoy playing games. Think about a time when you played a game with a friend or family member. Write a story to tell what happened one time when you played a game.

Expository

There are many things you can buy at the mall or at your favorite store. If you had all the money you needed, what would you buy? Write an essay to tell what you would buy and why you chose that item.

What is the best book you ever read? Think about why you liked that book the most. Write an essay to explain why you liked a particular book the most.

What is your favorite television program? Think about why you like that program the most. Write an essay to explain why a particular television program is your favorite.

What is your least favorite television program? Think about what you dislike about it the most. Write an essay to explain why you do not like this program.

Who is your favorite family member? Think about why this person is special to you. Write an essay to explain why this person is special to you.

What is your favorite game or activity to play outdoors? Think about why you like it so much. Write an essay to explain why this game or activity is your favorite.

Most kids have a favorite teacher. Think about a teacher you have had who was special to you. Write an essay to tell why that teacher was your favorite.

Do you have to help out at your house? Think about a job or chore that you do at home. Write an essay to tell why it is important for children to do a job or chore.

Many classrooms have classroom pets. Think about what would make a good pet for your classroom. Write an essay to explain why this is the best pet for your class to get.

Most students have objects that are special to them. Think about something that is really special to you. Write an essay to explain why a particular object is special to you.

Almost everyone has a favorite day of the week. Think about what you do on special days. Write an essay to tell why a particular day of the week is your favorite.

Everyone will agree that it is important to eat foods that keep us healthy. Think about why this is important. Write an essay to explain why it is important to eat foods that will help to keep us healthy.

All of you are in school to get an education. Think about why this is important. Write an essay to explain why it is important to go to school.

Most kids have a favorite place they like to go when they are at home. Think about your own home and where you like to be when you are there. Write an essay to explain why you like a special place in your house.

Children spend many hours in school, but most still have free time in the evenings or on weekends. Think about what you like to do when you are not at school. Write an essay to tell what you like to do and why you like that activity.

Most kids have favorite games they like to play. What is your favorite game? Write an essay to explain why a particular game is your favorite.

Descriptive

Most students have favorite outfits or pieces of clothing that they love. What types clothes or shoes are special to you? Write a description of a piece of clothing, a pair of shoes or an outfit that you really like.

Have you ever thought about an ideal place to live? Think about a house or unusual home that would be fun to live in. Write an essay to describe that place to live.

Think about an invention that would make your life easier. What would it look like and what could it do? Write an essay to describe an invention that would make your life easier.

Your dad asks you to take out the garbage. Just as you get to the curb, you see a bright green light and hear a loud noise. Write a description of what you are seeing and hearing.

There are many things you can buy at the mall or at your favorite store. If you had all the money you needed, what would you buy? Choose one item and then write a description of it.

Kids often have a favorite place they like to go in their neighborhood. Think about where you like to go in your own neighborhood. Write an essay to describe this special place in your neighborhood.

Animals do some very interesting things. Think about a time you watched an animal. Write a description of the animal and what it was doing.

Teachers like to make their classroom look special. Think about an ideal classroom. Write a description of what the best classroom could be like.

Almost everyone has a favorite storybook character. Who is yours? Write a description of your favorite storybook character.

Many stores have interesting displays in their windows. Think about a store window that you have seen or one that you think would be good to write about. Write a description of what was in the store window and how it made you feel.

Most kids like to travel. Think about a place you would like to go. Describe this place in such a way that the reader will understand what you like about it and why you want to go there.

Almost everyone has a favorite time of the year. Think about the seasons and how they change. Choose a special time of the year and write an essay to describe it.

Most students have objects that are special to them. Think about something that is really special to you. Write an essay to describe a special, particular object.

What comes to your mind when you hear the words, "This is awesome!" Think about a person, place, or object that make you think of this expression. Write a description to help the reader understand why "awesome" is the best way to describe that person, place, or object.

Most schools have a cafeteria. Think about what would make a school cafeteria great. Write an essay to describe the ideal school cafeteria.

Think about things in your life that are familiar. Select one thing that you know well. Describe it so clearly that the reader will understand all that you know about this one thing.

Choose a person, place, or object that you think is exciting. Think of all the things that make it exciting to you. Now write a description so that the reader will understand why that person, place, or object is so exciting.